Dream Big!

Anything IS Possible!

Rick Hoyt says:
"Yes, you Can!"

Go For it!

DESTINED
TO RUN:
My Spiritual Journey
from Couch Potato
to Ironman

Wes Harding

Requests for permission to make copies of any
part of the work should be submitted online
to toddcivin1@aol.com or mailed to:

Todd Civin
2 Robbins Road
Winchendon, MA 01475.

ISBN-10: 1620862670
ISBN-13: 9781620862674
CPSIA Code: PRB0313A

Library of Congress Control Number: 2013933795

Book design by Joshua Taggert

Printed in the United States

www.mascotbooks.com

Dedication

Destined to Run is dedicated to you, the reader. You are on a journey that travels through time and it is no accident that you are holding this book. It is my hope and prayer that the words you read in these pages will become an oasis of inspiration and encouragement to you. Dream big and seek out the adventures that life has to offer.

To my wonderful wife, Sue, who has put so much time and energy into my life (and into this book). You are the love of my life and together, we will go hand in hand to explore new lands and climb new mountains. You have completed my life and words will never be able to express my love and gratitude for all you do. Your belief in me has strengthened me so that, with God's help, we can do the impossible together.

To my four beautiful daughters: Rebekah, Jessica, Anissa, and Ciera. You truly have lit up my life. You have been my cheerleaders in life and have encouraged me to aim for the moon and pick up a few stars along the way. With cameras in hand, you have captured all those moments that will be remembered for a lifetime. Thank you. I will cherish all the memories of the times we spent together and I know that God has a great plan for your life. So dream big!

To my parents: Peter and Betty Harding, my heroes in life. Thank you for believing in me. You have been a constant source of unconditional love and support. The dreams I have experienced throughout this book would not have been possible without your belief that dreams do come true and that anything is possible. It is by your example you have left a legacy to the next generation and it is in your footsteps I will follow.

And finally, to my good friend and co-author of this book: Todd Civin. Without your encouragement and guidance, the dream of writing this book would have never come true. Not only did you see something in me, but you believed in me. I will always be indebted to your kindness and encouragement. I am glad that God allowed us to cross paths and share this journey together as we embark upon a new world. Although hundreds of miles separate us, you will always be a part of my family and there is always a light left on for you in our home.

Table of Contents

Preface: The Lagniappe

By: Todd Civin

> *"If the waiter in the restaurant stumbles and spills a gill of coffee down the back of your neck, he says 'For lagniappe, sah,' and gets you another cup without extra charge."*
>
> —*Mark Twain from Life on the Mississippi*

The word lagniappe (pronounced lanny-yap) is a French-Cajun word often heard in the Bayou region of Louisiana. It's a word that means "beyond full measure" or "to give a little extra." It is best described as the equivalent of giving someone a thirteenth ear of corn when they only pay for a dozen or what is commonly known as a Baker's dozen.

I learned about the word when writing a story about my friend Roger Crawford, a skilled athlete and motivational speaker, who shocked the world of collegiate tennis some years ago when he amassed a wins-loss record of 18-11 despite being born without arms and with only one leg. As you can imagine, Roger is a living, breathing example of the word lagniappe.

I use the word sparingly in my own personal vocabulary because there are very few who earn the respect of being associated with such an awesome word. So few, unfortunately, truly "give a little extra" in all that they do.

I met Wes Harding in April of 2012 while both of us served in differing capacities on the Team Hoyt Boston Marathon Team. I was working (and playing) as the Team's social media director while Wes was there to represent Team Hoyt as one of thirty runners hand-selected to run the 26.2 mile course from Hopkinton to Boston. What stood out most about Wes was his effervescent personality, his enthusiastic way of speaking, and the sense of warmth that emanated from his being. His journey from couch potato to marathon runner was shared with the team during our three days together, but was only one of thirty amazingly inspirational stories that the team members carried with them that weekend. See, one of the ways that Dick and

Rick Hoyt select their team members is through their heart, their dedication, and their ability to overcome obstacles and climb mountains. Wes' mountain was his weight and lack of health and fitness; a mountain he not only climbed but conquered. Like me, the nearly three dozen members of the Hoyt Team found Wes to be the life of the party and an inspiration to each of us.

Wes and I kept in touch over the course of the next six months and I assumed that I would see him once per year at Marathon time for as long as we both were honored enough to be considered a part of the exclusive Team. To my surprise, however, Wes invited me to make the trek from my home in Massachusetts to his home in Sarnia, Ontario, for the purpose of pedaling my first book, *One Letter at a Time*. I accepted Wes' invitation and spent four wonderful October days in Canada being entertained by Wes and his equally hospitable family. I frequented many of Wes' stomping grounds and heard literally dozens of stories from Wes' life, the same stories that you will read about between the covers of this book. At times, I felt as if I was on the "Peterman Reality Bus Tour" from *Seinfeld* fame as Wes took me physically and anecdotally through each amazingly entertaining neighborhood of his life.

It was during our time together that we both realized what Wes had to offer the world and made the decision to pen his motivational and inspirational stories to paper. I came to the conclusion that Wes' story was much more than just a story about a fat guy deciding to get healthy. It was instead the "lagniappe," a gift above and beyond expectation. A little bit more. Wes opens up his life and shares with the reader more incredible stories about defying odds and overcoming obstacles than any human being should have had to endure. Yet, as the reader will learn with the outcome of each saga, Wes continues to remain a step ahead of his challenges and escape unscathed and better off for it.

Over the course of the ensuing four weeks, he created *Destined to Run*, another example of his ability to over achieve. As I read a newly written chapter nearly every other day, I marveled at not only the quantity of work, but more importantly the quality of each tale this amazing storyteller was weaving. In true Wes fashion, he once again gave me the "lagniappe." With each sentence, each paragraph, and each chapter I am sure you will agree that he gave us a "little bit more" than we expected.

Foreword
By: Dick Hoyt

Destined to Run is a book about overcoming obstacles, perseverance, faith, love of family, and going from couch potato to Boston Marathon to Ironman. To that point, Wes Harding's life sounds a little like my life. But Wes has also had to overcome unimaginable heartache in his life and has literally had to rise from the ashes.

Wes's story is one that will make you laugh and have you cry. Wes is a very humble person and that comes out when you meet him in person and when you read his story.

I am proud to call Wes my fellow Boston Marathon teammate and my friend. Wes, you are a wonderful example and role model for the students in your school, as well as for everyone who has the opportunity to meet you. I know your book will inspire the next generation of couch potatoes to want to make something of their lives as well after reading your book.

THE WARMUP

Destined To Run is comprised of 140.6 miles or triumphs, struggles, and life stories. Why 140.6 miles, you may ask? As you may already know, 140.6 represents the distance of a full Ironman competition. Each mile marker brings a greater experience than the one before. For runners and triathletes, the thrill of the race is what brings them to the starting line. Some miles along the journey bring pain and suffering, while others promise hope and belief that anything is possible. Like an Ironman competition, this book reveals life's stories of pain and blessings that come from being determined. The stories in this book are aimed to not only encourage you, but also to inspire you to achieve your dreams and aspirations. You are never too old to dream big and reach for the stars. Anything is possible!

INTRODUCTION:

ANYTHING IS POSSIBLE

"We are judged by what we finish, not by what we started"

—*Anonymous*

IRONMAN – LAKE PLACID, NEW YORK: As I stood on the banks of Mirror Lake on that warm Sunday morning in July, the world around me seemed to echo my sentiment that *anything is possible*. The months of training leading up to this momentous endeavor I was about to embark upon had now come down to this very moment. Was it conceivable to achieve something you had been repeatedly reminded was not remotely possible? It was only a few years ago, as my clock ticked to forty years, that I found myself entrenched between the cushions of our overstuffed living room couch brushing Oreo crumbs off my belly, as I watched an Ironman competition on TV, thinking to myself that I would like to do that one day. The ultimate hypocrisy was watching, admiring, and fantasizing about these finely tuned athletes with bodies chiseled from the finest granite, while I slouched on our easy chair as an unmotivated, overweight, and depressed couch potato. I dipped another cookie into the crumb-filled glass of room temperature milk, popped it in my mouth, and shook the empty bag, hoping to find another row of cellophane-encased chocolate.

Fast forward to here and now, as I find myself perched on the shores of the crystal-clear lake in northern New York, elbow to elbow with thousands of bathing-cap-clad athletes, each preparing to spend the next three-quarters of a day in pursuit of realizing a dream and being dubbed an Ironman. A fleeting thought enters my mind. How deeply it disturbs me when some people dare to dream big and others try just as valiantly to douse their optimistic flame. My life was littered with several envious souls who told me that my dream of becoming an Ironman was unrealistic and impossible. Today, this very day, I had seventeen hours in which to prove them wrong and to prove to them that dreams can come true, if you believe hard enough.

The pristine lake looked perfectly calm and inviting as the sun peered over the mountaintops. It would be those very mountaintops that would later produce legs two and three of my challenge, as we would ride 112 miles through the Adirondack Mountain range, followed by a grueling 26.2-mile marathon run. Those events were on the horizon, but the challenge that rested at my fingertips was a 2.4-mile swim that would commence in just minutes. Each one of us has experienced events in our lives that altered the very fiber of who we are as human beings. I knew, before the cannon ever sounded, that this event would be one of those life-changing experiences that would challenge me physically, mentally, spiritually, and emotionally. The quest to become one of the elite—an Ironman—would challenge my very core, push me beyond my comfort level, and summon me to heights I had never reached before.

I remember glancing down at my watch as the time approached 6:50 AM. Ten minutes remained until I took my first stroke into the renowned Lake Placid. With the speakers blaring U2's hit "Beautiful

Day," I remember saying out loud, yet to myself, that it was going to be just that: a beautiful day. Bono's epic anthem would keep me company throughout the day as the lyrics resonated in my head during nearly every stroke, every pedal, and every step over the next thirteen-plus hours.

Mike Riley, the well-recognized voice of Ironman, asked the very question I had been rehearsing the answer for during the past year of training: "Who wants to become an Ironman, today?"

Over 2,800 competitors cheered and shouted at the top of their collective lungs in unison the same inspired two words, "I do!" With my heart visibly beating through my now-chiseled chest, I bid farewell to my family who now stood with me on the shores of the sandy beach. I took my first step into the refreshing water. The next time I would see my family-turned-cheering-section would be that magical number—140.6 miles later.

As confident as my fellow would-be-Ironmen seemed, I knew we were all wrestling with the same giants: the giants of fear and self-doubt. The Ironman fear can be down-right overwhelming, at times, both during training and during the actual event. How will this body, this mind, and this spirit ever survive after it puts itself through 140.6 miles of torture? We are each overflowing, at times, with self-doubt as we wonder what on earth we have gotten ourselves into. We were all there for the same purpose: to conquer our fears and perform what seems to be impossible, achieving the status of Ironman. We all knew, as we waited in anticipation for the cannon to sound, that once you commit, there is no turning back. Seldom does a person get the opportunity to experience the amazing exhilaration of conquering their own fears and apprehensions, but today we were all becoming authors: the authors of our own destiny.

Not one to do anything in moderation, be it the inhalation of chocolate, the love of my wife and daughters, or the admiration of our Lord and Savior, I swam out through the shoulder-to-shoulder crowd of competitors, squeezing myself through literally hundreds of wetsuit-clad would-be-Ironmen to the starting line. The race was about to begin. As "Beautiful Day" continued to blast from the loud speakers, I knew this was going to be a beautiful day, and I was not going to let it escape my grasp! I had never felt such a sense of life. My heart beat in anticipation, and for the minutes leading up to the sounding of the cannon, my whole life flashed before me. Frame by frame, I recounted all the highs and lows of my forty-four years on the planet. My mental journey through my life was suddenly interrupted with the fearful question that haunted me, "Can I do this?" After all, it was just three months ago I did what seemed impossible to that point—I ran the Boston Marathon as a qualified runner at the age of forty-four, something that people said would never happen for me. Not only did I run the Boston Marathon, but I ran it with my heroes, Dick and Rick Hoyt of Team Hoyt. The final words that projected onto the blank canvas of my mind as the cannon sounded was, "Wes, You Can!" an adaptation of the Hoyt's inspirational mantra of "Yes, You Can."

The road of life twists and turns, and no two directions taken ever produce the same outcome. Our greatest rewards can be found in staying true to our course. The goal and intent of this book is not solely to share stories of the many obstacles I have been forced to battle through and conquer, but to inspire and motivate readers, to encourage the understanding and belief that *yes, you can* do anything you want, and that dreams do come true. This is my story.

MILE 1

THE DREAM BEGINS

> "All our dreams can come true—if we have the courage to pursue them"
>
> —*Walt Disney*

The gates were just opening as I entered the mall, which was filled with post-Christmas sales and shoppers with returns in hand. I really hoped to impress the sales woman as I entered the shoe store that Monday morning. She approached me gingerly and asked if she could help me as I browsed the countless colors and makes of running shoes. Christmas was just a few days in the rear-view mirror, and I was now tipping the scales at 220 with gusts up to 225 pounds. I had slowly but surely become an overweight couch potato, who had accomplished very little in life while climbing the proverbial "age mountain." I had just turned forty a few weeks before and had come to the realization that, if I was lucky, my life was now half over. I wasn't over the hill, but I could certainly see the top, and the other side of the mountain didn't look very pretty from where I stood. The first forty years had some highlights, but

I found myself surrounded by a sense of unfilled dreams that left me wanting. For the first time in my life, I had made the conscious decision to make changes, to start "living the dream," and making a difference in the years I had left. I was determined to change my life, and I knew as I entered this store that this was my moment to stand on the podium of life and finally announce to the world my dream of running a marathon.

Up to this point, the only thing I over-achieved at in life was eating. I, like the Hoyt's, subscribed to the mantra of "Yes, You Can," but for me, that sentiment was followed by phrases like, "*Yes, you can* super-size that order," "*Yes, you can* pass me the gravy," and "*Yes, you can* give me an extra scoop of ice cream on my banana split sundae." Eating was something I did well. It was something I enjoyed, and it was something in which I found comfort. However, it brought with it something I did not desire: an increase in poundage, a mounting feeling of low self-esteem, and a sense of depression. Every morning, I would leap from my bed, jump on the scale, and watch the needle steadily rise. I justified my weight gain by saying that I would lose it one day, but that day was nowhere in sight.

Not only had I become overweight due to poor eating choices, but I was also physically inactive, as well. The outdoors, yard work, or anything that exerted any amount of energy was off my list. In fact, I often joked that the only time I burned calories was walking back and forth from the table to the all-you-can-eat buffet. I had become unhappy with myself. My confidence and self-image was eroding with each breath I took. I knew the path I was on was not the one I wanted to be on. In fact, I wanted to get off the metaphorical treadmill and knew that the time was now. I needed to make a change, and I needed to do it right then.

And who would be a better person to share my dream with than this particular saleslady, who I knew to be a well-respected marathon runner and running coach in our community. This icon of a runner was someone who people admired and looked up to. I was here in this store for one reason, and for one reason only: to begin my pursuit of a dream, and I needed a good pair of running shoes to catapult me off the couch and to bring me one step closer to that dream. It had been said that the hardest part of running a marathon was taking the first step, and here I was, taking the first step inside this shoe store. My dream had begun, and this was my time!

The dream of running a marathon had been born many years before today. There are certain moments in life that, for whatever reason, become an indelible part of our memory. We miraculously remember the when, where, and why, or the birth of a thought, and that thought remains with us like an itch needing to be scratched. As a young child of eight years old, I remember sitting in our living room, watching the Boston Marathon on TV and thinking, *I want to do that one day*. The thought of being on television and in front of a half-million spectators lining the streets thrilled me to no end, and I thought of this on many occasions over the next three decades. Watching the runners as they took their mark in the historic village of Hopkinton, Massachusetts, and then battling each other through the streets of eastern Massachusetts, before taking the gradual descent into Newton, intrigued me. Though I was a born-and-bred Canadian, I longed to visit Boston at some point in my life and imagined that my visit to the land of Paul Revere and John Hancock would be while I was clad in running shorts and a pair of New Balance running shoes. I remember the commentators talking about "Heartbreak Hill" and watching the runners struggle up that perfectly placed piece of topography, before finally entering Boston in front of hundreds of thousands of screaming spectators. It seemed that the Boston Marathon was the runners' nirvana—the ultimate achievement. I knew that was the race I wanted to do someday, but assumed that it would take place closer to age twenty-four than age forty-four. Even at that young age, not wanting to do anything in moderation, I dreamed big! The dream of running the Boston Marathon was planted at that tender age.

I turned and looked at the saleslady to answer her question of how she could assist me. I told her that I was there because I needed a good pair of running shoes. She asked me what I was planning to do with those shoes. As a non-runner and a first time customer in the store, I found her question quite strange, but I was ready to accept her challenge.

I always believed that you are the author of your own destiny, and it was my time to declare my destiny to her. I proudly stated to her that, "I am going to run a marathon!" I paused for a moment, allowing her to ingest the announcement of my intentions. She didn't seem to react, so in order to really impress this woman I added, "And I am going to run the Boston Marathon." This was, after all, my dream, to run the greatest marathon in the world and after all, dreams do come true. I knew my destiny was waiting for me. This was my day to begin.

The sales woman examined me from head to toe. She looked me up and down like a drill sergeant inspecting a troop. As I stood waiting for her words of encouragement, she slapped me with a dose of reality that I really was not expecting. The next five words that came from her lips literally changed my life. The look in her eyes pierced my inner soul as she blurted point blank, "You will never run a marathon!"

I stood there in total amazement, trying to comprehend the meaning of her eye-opening statement. I would never run a marathon? How could this be? With that quintet of loosely strung-together syllables, this running coach, marathon runner, and expert in the running field had chewed me up and spit me out like a piece of overcooked cube steak. Her words destroyed an inner feeling that resided so beautifully in my heart just moments before, and now all thoughts of running a marathon seemed to instantly fade. After all, she was the expert, right? She was likely able to look at my grossly out-of-shape physique and immediately determine that I was incapable of accomplishing such a feat of commitment and athletic endurance. I immediately felt like a schoolboy standing against the brick wall of the school building, while the roster for kickball was being selected. While each budding all-star was chosen before me, I remained against the wall, deemed unworthy of contributing positively to the game. Once again, I was to be selected last, if at all. As she turned to wait on another customer, I imagined the nods of agreement from the nearby customers. As a wounded bird about to take its last breath, I felt the dream die, as I sauntered out of the store carrying nothing but my withered sense of pride.

I walked out to my car with the pain of realizing that she was probably right. I would never run a marathon. I mean, who was I kidding? I was an overweight couch potato, and overweight couch potatoes do not run marathons! With my head hanging lower than my oversized mid-section, my sadness turned to anger. *Where is God in all this?* I thought. I always knew that God had a plan for my life, and I knew that, according to Jeremiah 29:11, God had a plan to prosper me and not to harm me. I knew His plan was to give me hope and a future, but where was the future now? My hope of ever running a marathon had died in that store. I cried out to God to answer me, but He was silent, eerily silent. I heard nothing.

I went home that night and had a pity party for myself. "Woe is me," I cried out to God, as I felt that running the Boston Marathon would never happen for me, and for good reason. I was a non-runner who was stuck in a rut. I knew that before you could even run the Boston Marathon you had to qualify for it, and with Boston's strict qualification times, very few marathon runners ever achieved that goal. As silly as it may seem, it never even dawned on me to alter my goal and to simply run a 5K, or even do a sit-up. I was focused on someday running Boston, and after being harpooned by the store clerk, this whale, washed up on the shores of Nantucket Beach, wasn't thinking especially clearly.

Like a skipping record-player, the words "You will never run a marathon" played over and over in my mind during the days that followed. This dark cloud of despair now hung over my head. My self-confidence had been shattered, and the dream of running the world's oldest annual marathon would remain just a childhood fantasy. The following days were accompanied by a greater feeling of hopelessness. Each day, I would cry out to God and ask *why*, as I spiraled into depression and negative thinking. God remained silent. I continually asked myself if my dream was even realistic to begin with. Was I thinking like an over-achiever, wanting to run this race when so few runners in the world actually accomplish it? In my anger, I began to wonder why God had ever placed this dream within me, when He knew it was impossible for me to accomplish. I knew the power of God; I had seen and experienced it firsthand before, but currently He was not felt or heard. I found myself blaming God for the destruction of this dream. I knew that God spoke in a still, small voice, but I was not hearing Him.

As Sunday approached, I found myself not wanting to go to church, and I thought, for good reason. How could one worship God when He seemed so distant? In hindsight, what I didn't know at the time was that God was waiting for me there. As I arrived at church with my family that morning, I noticed in the program that our pastor's sermon was on setting goals. It was that time of year when the world makes New Year's resolutions for the upcoming year. I knew this sermon would be the same old war cry that we hear every year at this time; it is time to set new goals for the New Year. I continued my streak of negative thinking and immediately came to the conclusion that talk is cheap. As a visual learner, I have always found myself saying, "I would much rather see a sermon than hear one." I wanted to see someone live out a sermon for a change.

As the sermon began, my mind immediately wandered back to the shoe store incident from only days earlier. The words "You will never run a marathon" echoed in my mind. I was trapped, haunted by these words. It seemed that the ghosts of despair were everywhere. I could only imagine what it would be like to do what now seemed impossible— to run a marathon. At that moment, the lights in the auditorium dimmed. The congregation was about to watch a video surely intended to hammer home the pastor's sermon. What I didn't know was that God was about to work in my life. He was about to change my way of thinking and, ultimately, about to change my life forever!

As the parishioners gazed intently at the screen, I witnessed an individual in a wheelchair, obviously paralyzed from the neck down. He was tapping his head diligently on some sort of a communication device. He seemed to be trying to spell something. A million questions ran instantly through my mind as I wondered who this individual was and what he was attempting to spell. The song that was being played in the background haunted me. Its title "I Can Only Imagine," performed by Christian rock band Mercy Me, had captured my attention. The letters this disabled individual was spelling on his communication device captivated me. I was absolutely mesmerized as the word "C-A-N" appeared across the screen. I pondered the thought. *Could it be that this is a message from God? Is God talking to me directly and using this man in the video to share his message with me?*

I watched intently, hands on my chin, as the video told the story of an incredibly loving family interacting with a child who was disabled and apparently unable to control his body from the neck down. Then I saw it: a father pulling a boat with his son in it. Obviously, this father-and-son team was in some sort of athletic competition. I soon realized that they were competing in a triathlon. As I watched this father carry his paralyzed son through the transition area and then place him on his bike, incredible feelings of determination, dedication, and love started to well up inside of me. I thought to myself, *This father must love his son so much that he is willing to go to the extreme for him.* As the father and son then started the biking portion of the race, my heart started to pound. It was as if God Himself was knocking on the door of my heart, trying to get my attention. As I watched this father biking through the mountaintops with his son on the front of the bike, I knew God was talking to me. Absolutely amazing, I thought to myself as I watched this paralyzed son smile into the camera. Life was obviously good for him, but he was paralyzed. How could this be? It seemed to me that this son was living out his dreams with his father. God now had my undivided attention!

As I watched this incredible father push his severely disabled son in the running portion of the race, the words "I can only imagine" flooded my mind as Mercy Me's lyrics reiterated that sentiment. Tears welled as I watched the two heroes cross the finish line together with thousands of spectators cheering wildly for them. To see them achieve this incredible feat on the screen before me left me motionless and speechless. They were living out their dreams together! What an incredible story of a father's love for his son. And then it hit me. I was stunned as the still, small voice of God spoke to my heart at that moment. The voice I was familiar with and longed to hear, but the voice had been so disturbingly silent up to this point. Through this video, God said to me, "*Yes, you can* live out your dreams. We will do it together. A father and a son performing the impossible!"

When I arrived home after church that afternoon, I fell to my knees and asked God to forgive me. Here I was with two perfectly working legs, two good arms, and a mind filled with ambition and adventure, and I was continuing to bathe in self-pity. How foolish and selfish I had been to think that I had it bad. I had doubted God's power and love. It was at that very moment that my life changed. God then brought to my mind a quote by the late Steve Jobs from his commencement speech delivered at Stanford University in 2005. In this incredible speech, Jobs said, "Your time is limited, so don't waste it living someone else's life. Don't be trapped by dogma—which is living with the results of other people's thinking. Don't let the noise of other's opinions drown out your own inner voice. And most important, have the courage to follow your heart and intuition. They somehow already know what you truly want to become. Everything else is secondary."

I realized that the only place where your dreams become impossible is in your own thinking. As I buried my self-doubt and the voices of the other people in my mind, I became something that day: I became a new person. It did not matter what other people thought. It only mattered what God thought, and like this amazing father and son team, God said, "Yes, you can!"

As a non-runner, overweight, underachiever, it was time for me to get my new pair of running shoes and start on the journey all over again. But this time it would be different. I realized that my conditions were less than perfect, but God reassured me not to wait until everything is just right. It would never be perfect. I realized in that moment that there will always be challenges, always be obstacles to overcome, and likely less-than-perfect conditions. God assured me that with each step I took, I would grow stronger and stronger, increasingly self-confident, and ultimately successful. It was now time for me to start living the dream and pursue my dreams.

Boston, here I come!

MILE 10

THE INSPIRATION:
THE HOYTS

It's a boy! The dream of having a family had now begun for Dick and Judy Hoyt; their first son had been brought into their lives. This baby was a gift from God. Dick had always wanted children. In fact, he wanted lots of them. Little did the Hoyts know at that time that this little baby boy, born on January 10, 1962, was not only going to drastically change their lives, but was going to change and inspire the world, as well. Born in Winchester Hospital near Boston, Massachusetts, the Hoyts were overjoyed in becoming parents for the very first time. They had prepared for this day for months. It was their time to celebrate!

Their son's name would be Richard Eugene Hoyt, Jr., named after his father. But that name was called into question when tragedy struck during the birthing process. It was mid-morning when Richard was born. His father was at work when he received the call from the hospital informing him that his wife had just given birth to a baby boy. This was great news to the ears of Dick Hoyt, the elder, who was only twenty-one years old at the time. But the good news soon turned into news of concern when the doctors continued to tell Dick that there were complications during the birthing process. This news came unexpectedly for Dick and, of course, for Judy. Although his wife was doing fine, his son was not. His newborn son was in great distress.

Richard was an active baby while in the womb, and while he was being born he apparently somehow got himself turned around just minutes before his birth. Unfortunately for the Hoyts, these were the days before monitors. If the doctors had realized the position Richard was in, it would have been a whole different story for them and for the world. During Richard's excited entry into the world, his umbilical cord became wrapped around his neck, which technically strangled him. Even though the doctors tried desperately to untangle the cord as quickly as they could, the deprivation of oxygen to Richard's brain caused irreparable damage.

After days of tests, the doctors met with the Hoyts and informed them of the severity of Richard's birth defects. There were doubts that Richard would even survive, and if he did, he would live his life with severe disabilities. With so many questions and no answers, the Hoyts were left wondering why this had to happen to their son. What was to become of him? They felt so alone. Dick's wife, Judy, after receiving the news of the fate of their son, asked Dick if he still wanted to name their firstborn son after him. "You bet your life I do," he told his wife. His name would be Rick, and regardless of his disability, he would carry his father's name.

After nearly eight months of prayer, hope, and belief, the Hoyts were finally informed that their son had cerebral palsy. *Cerebral* refers to the cerebrum, which is the affected area of the brain, and *palsy* refers to disorder of movement. In simple terms it actually means brain paralysis, and during the time when oxygen was deprived to Richard's brain, the section that controls muscles and motor activity was damaged. This damage would leave Rick as a non-verbal, spastic quadriplegic.

Life for this baby would be different; he would not be like the other boys and girls. In fact, according to the doctors, his life would amount to nothing. In his book *Devoted*, Dick Hoyt states that when the diagnosis was officially made for their son, the best advice their doctors could give them was, "put Rick in an institution. Forget about him. Don't visit. Don't think about him. Go on with your life." The doctors continued to advise the Hoyts that their son would be nothing more than a vegetable. Dick's dream of playing baseball or hockey with his son died on that day. His son would remain in a wheelchair for the rest of his life. Dick and Judy had to make a decision that day, a decision that would change the course of history.

The choice of either putting Rick away for the rest of his life or to take him home was not a difficult one for the Hoyts. In fact, they did not even have to think about it. Their answer was *no*. Their hearts' cries would be for their son. Rick would be brought home, loved, and brought up like any other child. Dick and Judy knew it would not be easy, but this was their calling. Dick knew in his heart that his son was just as special as any other child, and he would be willing to journey a thousand miles for him. Little did Dick know that one day he would literally do that for his son; they would do it together!

Sometimes life brings you to such crossroads that you feel smiling is far better than crying. Life for Dick and Judy Hoyt would be radically changed, and so would the lives of thousands of others, because of Rick's existence and the choices that he and the Hoyts would make throughout his lifetime. Over the next few years, the Hoyts were met with feelings of denial, anger, confusion, and bitterness, but with each passing day, they could see that their son was special. Their emotions would soon be transformed into a bond that would be a testimonial to the rest of the world, a bond the world so desperately needed to see and experience. Both Judy and Dick knew that their son was unique and set apart for a higher calling, but it was difficult to see what that calling would be. Still, they believed.

The Hoyts later had two other boys who would become a source of strength and encouragement to both Rick and his parents. Rick was one of their sons, and though he was different than brothers Rob and Russell, whatever the family did, so did Rick. Dick and Judy would take Rick sledding and swimming and even taught him the alphabet and basic words, like any other child. Rick was not excluded from anything, but rather a valuable member of the family. One of the greatest challenges the Hoyts faced was communicating with Rick and vice versa. They knew Rick was intelligent, but they needed to find a way for Rick to communicate with the rest of the world.

Then it happened, in 1972, when Rick was ten-years-old, a breakthrough came in the area of assistive technology. Computers were just starting to be developed, and a skilled group of engineers at Tufts University in Boston, Massachusetts, built an interactive computer especially for Rick, after the Hoyts raised the incredible sum of $5,000 to have it developed. This machine would be dubbed "The Hope Machine." This crude looking computer consisted of a cursor, which was used to highlight every letter of the alphabet. Once the letter Rick wanted was highlighted, he was able to select it by just a simple tap with his head against a head piece attached to his wheelchair. When the computer was originally brought home, Rick surprised everyone with his first words. Instead of saying, "Hi, Mom," or "Hi, Dad," Rick's first "spoken" words were, "Go, Bruins!" The Boston Bruins were in the Stanley Cup finals that season, and it was clear from that moment on that Rick loved sports and followed the game just like anyone else. This machine had opened up a whole new world for Rick. He had now gained his independence and proved his intelligence.

The Hoyts fought to integrate Rick into the public school system, pushing administrators and educators to see beyond Rick's physical limitations. In fact, Rick's mother would be a pioneer in changing the field of education. Inclusion was unheard of in those days, but the Hoyts felt that all children, regardless of their exceptionalities or disabilities, should have the right to attend public school. After many years of writing letters and petitioning the government, Rick was allowed to go to public school. Because of Judy's efforts, the governor of Massachusetts signed the Bartley-Daly Act, more commonly known as Chapter 766. This chapter allowed countless children with disabilities to be educated in public schools alongside their non-disabled siblings, friends, and peers.

In the spring of 1977, when Rick was fifteen years old, he told his father that he wanted to participate in a 5-mile benefit run for a lacrosse player who had been paralyzed in an accident. Far from being a long-distance runner, his father had agreed to push Rick in his wheelchair, and they finished all 5 miles, coming in next-to-last. That night, Rick told his father through his computer, "Dad, when I'm running, it feels like I'm not handicapped." Those words moved Dick Hoyt more than any he had ever heard. This would be the beginning of a father/son team, which would become known around the world as Team Hoyt. This team would go on to do over 1,000 races, including marathons, duathlons, and triathlons (six of them being Ironman competitions). Also adding to their list of achievements would be biking across the United States in 1992, completing a full 3,735 miles in forty-five consecutive days. On October 11, 2008, both Dick and Rick were inducted into the Ironman Hall of Fame at the 2008 Ford Ironman World Championship in Kona, Hawaii, with Rick being the first special needs athlete to earn such an honor. In 2012, Dick and Rick Hoyt ran their thirtieth Boston Marathon, a feat few people in the world have ever accomplished. Over the years, the two have established themselves as integral parts of the lore that is the Boston Marathon.

Rick Hoyt's brother, Rob, said it best when he said, "I sometimes wonder how anybody can complain about life's inequities or insurmountable challenges after witnessing first-hand what Rick endures on a daily basis." It is hard to complain, when we begin to take our eyes off ourselves and start looking at those around us.

That was exactly my problem. I was doing a lot of "navel gazing." Life revolved around me, and my problems always seemed bigger than anyone else's. I constantly found myself complaining about something or getting the raw end of the deal. My weight, my age, my profession, or anything I could find as an excuse justified my inability to make a difference. I often heard my wife saying to me, "You know, you whine too much." My "poor me" attitude had me trapped, and I needed an attitude change, and I needed it quickly.

One of the big problems I had was that I often found myself slipping into thinking of myself as the victim, believing I had little or no control over my life. In this mindset, I started to feel sorry for myself. In my negative view of life, I saw things as if the world was against me, and I was stuck in a land of sadness and self-pity. I wanted out of this mindset, and I wanted to start living an abundant life. It took a person like Rick Hoyt to demonstrate to me that even if life gives you lemons, it's time to make some lemonade. I needed to start thanking God for the things I did have, rather than complain and long for the things I did not have. I needed to develop an attitude of gratitude. I needed to turn my focus outward and start helping others, and I needed to start respecting myself.

Once I learned to stop focusing on all my problems and the things I did not have, I started to find joy in the simple things of life, and life was miraculously much better than it had been. I realize that life did not change at all, but my view of that life had changed immeasurably—the old glass half-full/half-empty principal. The amount of liquid in the glass doesn't change an iota, but the way we view the glass changes immensely. I look back now and realize it took an individual like Rick to show me that I am indeed blessed. It was only when I sought God and asked Him to forgive me that I realized the freedom I had at my fingertips, because, indeed, the world was mine. It was at that moment, in His small, still voice, God said to me, through the poem "God Forgive Me When I Whine" by Red Foley, that I needed to start looking around at the things I do have.

The world was mine! I know that God has created me in His image and by His hand. He has made me unique and special in my own way, so God forgive me when I whine. In his book entitled *One Letter at a Time*, Rick Hoyt says it best when he says, "I believe God had everything to do with the way my birth came out. The Bible says God planned our life even before we are born. When my umbilical cord wrapped around my neck, I believe it was part of God's plan. No one knew his plan, however, I think his plan is working out pretty well for me. Sometimes I do not like being this way, but then again, there are people who are in far worse shape than me."

As I have learned through Rick Hoyt, it is all a matter of perspective. We are indeed truly blessed once we start counting our many blessings and naming them one by one. Once this occurs, we truly realize how good we have it. It is time we that celebrate the goodness of God and look at ourselves through His eyes, rather than through the eyes of others. Before we complain about our own life, it's time we take a walk in someone else's shoes, or take a ride in their wheelchair.

I have learned many lessons by witnessing the Hoyts: sacrificial love, determination, perseverance, and dedication to their own message, but the greatest lesson I learned is that "Yes, You Can." *Yes, you can* overcome the obstacles that might come your way. This is the Hoyts' message, and it applies to not only the disabled, or the overweight, or runners, or couch potatoes. It applies to all of us. No matter who or what we are, we are faced with obstacles that at times seem insurmountable, but as stated earlier, it is our perspective when viewing those obstacles that determine our ability to achieve. I am always reminded that when we are surrounded by what appears to be many difficulties, we may in fact be surrounded by many opportunities. The Hoyts are a great example of this. Regardless of the opposition and roadblocks in life, you can do it.

Dare to dream, and watch the impossible happen. The world is mine! So with all my weight, inability to run, and all my baggage, I say…let the dream begin!

MILE 20

THE FIRST STEP:
LET THE DREAM BEGIN

"Twenty years from now you will be more disappointed by the things that you didn't do than by the ones you did do. So throw off the bowlines. Sail away from the safe harbor. Catch the trade winds in your sails. Explore. Dream. Discover."

—*Mark Twain*

"You're not going out in that snowstorm, are you?" my wife, Sue, inquired as I slipped on my running shoes.

It was late in the evening, and the snow was beckoning people to stay indoors. The north wind blew across the perfectly flat terrain of Sarnia, Ontario, and it was beginning to howl like a pack of wolves on a full-moon night. I was determined to start my dream, regardless of the forces of nature. Nothing was going to hold me back. I had made over forty years' worth of excuses and was going to leave that behavior behind me. It was time for me to set my sails and catch the trade winds to a new world.

"Yes, I am," I responded confidently.

It was just days before New Year's Day, and I knew I had to start my dream sometime and somewhere. I bundled myself in the warmest of clothes, laced up my shoes and bid farewell to my family as I headed for the door.

"You sure you want to do this?" my daughter Rebekah asked.

"It looks slippery out there!" added Jessica.

As I peered out the window into what seemed like a dark abyss, I knew this was my time to shine like the bright Canadian full moon that shone overhead. This was my big moment: a moment that would be forever etched in my mind. This step would mark the first step of a thousand miles to come.

I had decided earlier that day that I could not bring myself to run during daylight hours, but rather I'd start running under the cover of darkness, because I was so embarrassed that anyone would see me, and for good reason. Seeing an overweight guy wobbling down the road like a Weeble wobbling would not be a pretty sight. This night was perfect: no traffic, no people, no dogs, no one but me and my dream. As I walked out the front door, I took one last look at the thermometer. It was -15 degrees Celsius. I knew this would be hard in the most perfect of conditions, but the weather was not helping. As I pushed through the front door, the last words I heard coming from the house were, "We will keep the outside light on for you, just in case you want to turn back." Though I knew the family meant well, even they had doubts as to whether or not I would commit to this. I assume they expected me to come panting back through the front door by the time I had made it to the corner and back.

But there was no turning back. As I walked down the front steps, I saw them all: my four teenage daughters, my wife, and our dog, all peering through the front window. It was a sight they had never seen before; I was about to embark on a new adventure, and they did not want to miss it. I knew at that moment that my family would soon become my greatest cheerleaders. It would be their encouragement that would keep the dream alive, if ever I stumbled or faltered. They had heard about this idea for days, and now the appointed time had come to take the initial step.

I always love how God plants an idea as a seed and over time, waters that seed until it germinates. He uses others to encourage us and shine the sun upon that seed. He also gives us real-life examples to follow, blow wind upon and strengthen the seed; over time, those words blossom into a dream. This is particularly true in my case. For the past several months, a friend of mine in our church came up to me each Sunday and encouraged me to start running. I had always thought that running was dumb, and I often wondered if he had lost his mind. Besides, running involved too much energy and effort. It was hard work, I told myself. But something was unusual about my friend's encouragement, for he, too, was overweight, and he was doing something to make a change in his life. As I watched him each week, I began to notice a difference in his attitude, in his shape, and in his outlook on life. He seemed happier. In fact, he started to look much younger. I also noticed that he was becoming much thinner. Each Sunday, instead of commenting on the sermon, I found myself commenting on Kevin's radical change; he was losing weight, and he was starting to look good. Could it be that I was actually "seeing a sermon" taking place right before my eyes?

Then I heard it. One Sunday after Kevin had been running for quite some time, he came up to me and said the *M-word*. My ears perked up as if someone had just called my name; no one says the M-word. And then he said it again. He was going to run a marathon! He continued confirming his words of fate by saying that he was going to run the Marine Corps Marathon in Washington, DC. I was stunned. He was going to run a marathon? A marathon in Washington, DC?

I was ecstatic for him! I had never known anyone before who had ever run a distance that far. I was captivated by Kevin's dream. Not only had I seen a change in my friend's personality and outlook on life, but also in his weight loss and in his physical fitness. Kevin had demonstrated to me that it was possible to lose weight by running, and with proper diet to start to achieve the seemingly impossible. As icing on the cake, I watched Kevin drop from 240 pounds to 185 pounds. He was a completely different person, and he was the same age as I was: forty years old.

Soon after, on the day of his race, I logged onto the U.S. Marine Corps' website to watch Kevin's progress. I was amazed at the sheer number of people running that marathon, a number that I could not comprehend. I found myself cheering aloud from the comfort of my own couch as I watched Kevin do the impossible. He finished that marathon with a time of 4 hours, 46 minutes, and 50 seconds (4:46:50), coming in 10,518th place. *Simply amazing,* I thought to myself. And it was at that moment that I wanted what he had. I wanted to experience my dream of running a marathon and do the impossible. Kevin had done something for me that no one had ever done. Not only had he planted the idea of running a marathon, he watered that idea by encouraging me, and most importantly, he nurtured it by living it out. He was my visual example of what could be done. As an old proverb says, "The man who has confidence in himself gains the confidence of others." Kevin had the confidence and, in that, he built up confidence in me.

As I took my first step outside the door, my foot sank into the snow, as if to say, "Not tonight." But there would be no turning back. As I reached the end of the driveway, all of my 220 pounds screamed at me, as if to say it was time to turn around and enjoy the comforts of my couch. I looked down at my watch and set the time. How far was I going to run? No one knew, not even me. I just knew I wanted to lose all my weight in one night, so I would be the master of my distance and the master of my own destiny.

As I headed face first into the north wind, I could hear the clapping of the branches, as if they were screaming, "Well done, Harding, keep running, don't stop!" The sound of the crunching snow under my feet was a sweet sound. With each step, it reminded me that I am alive, that I am free indeed. The road to the Boston Marathon had begun.

As I reached the shore line of our lake, I could feel my lungs screaming at me to stop. The burning sensation of the cold wind told me enough is enough. It was time to put this silly idea to rest. It is funny that sometimes our greatest setbacks come from our own thinking. Our self-defeating behavior is like a poison, preventing us from achieving the things that we want in our own lives. We often sabotage ourselves by giving in to our own thinking. As I turned the corner and headed west, I found I was talking to myself. I told myself to, "Get out of the way," for I was coming through. I was glad at that moment that no one was around. It was crazy enough to run in a snowstorm, and talking to myself would be grounds for placing me in a psychiatric hospital.

As I rounded the next corner, I kept reminding myself aloud, "You can do this, you can do this." My legs, my heart, and my lungs were all telling me otherwise, but I continued. I was determined not to walk, and I was determined not to quit. I envisioned the Hoyts' video and told myself that one day, I want to run with them. As the letters C-A-N appeared in my mind, I knew I could do this. It was as if God was running right beside me, reminding me that we can do this together. With the wind now at my back, I could see my house and the light on the porch that was lit ever so brightly on that cold, dark, December night. That light became my beacon of hope to tell me that I was almost finished. I knew I could do it. The pain, the numbness, the tiredness would be my trophy that night.

As I stepped on my porch, I realized I had done it! I had run over 5 kilometers that night without quitting. I physically reached over my tired shoulder with my right arm and patted myself on the back. That moment was one of the greatest moments I have ever experienced. As I walked through the front door, my cheerleaders were waiting for me. They had a million questions for me, asking about my emotional experience and, through their smiles, I knew we were about to explore new lands together as a result of my new obsession. The most pertinent question they were dying to hear me answer was, "So, are you going to do this again?"

That answer was simple. "Yes." Whether or not they foresaw the length of road ahead that moment wasn't clear, but that night would forever change our family and the direction we were heading.

As I look back on that night, I realize it changed me. It helped me discover that it is not about how much you weigh or what you have done in your past, it is about what you are doing. Our bodies are amazing. I shouldn't have been able to run over 5 kilometers that night, but my body kept going as a result of my heart and my spirit. There is something about pushing yourself beyond your limits that people need to do at least once in their life. I know that twenty years from now I will be more disappointed by the things that I didn't do than by the ones I tried and failed at. I know with dreams there will be hurdles to climb, obstacles to go through, and disappointments to overcome, but I have no regrets on doing what I did that night. People need to take that one chance, that one time to see what they are capable of doing, and once they do, they are never the same. I love what the author of Hebrews says in Hebrew 12:1, "Do you see what this means—all these pioneers who blazed the way, all these veterans cheering us on? It means we'd better get on with it. Strip down, start running—and never quit!" (*The Message*).

I also learned that night that it doesn't matter what people think. It doesn't even matter if they think you can't do something. It only matters to you, and once you do it, you are never the same. Explore, dream, and discover what is waiting for you out there. Arthur Schopenhauer, a German philosopher, said it best when he said, "Every truth passes through three stages before it is recognized. In the first, it is ridiculed. In the second, it is opposed. In the third, it is regarded as self-evident." The greatest joy is realizing that *yes, you can* achieve the dreams that God has given to you.

Okay, God, let's do it together! Boston is 26.2 miles long! This is going to be the new me.

MILE 30

UNCOVERING THE NEW ME

"Do not worry if you have built your castles in the air. They are where they should be. Now put the foundations under them."

—*Henry David Thoreau*

"You're not having another bag of chips, are you?" Sue asked me as I ripped the top off yet another bag of sour cream and onion chips, right before bedtime.

"But, eating potatoes is good for you," I chirped back, knowing full well that this is the same argument I would make when I tried to convince her that candy corn is a vegetable, and there are milk and eggs in cake, so it must be a hardy breakfast item. I scoop another handful of chips and shove them down my pie hole, crunching them extra loud as I waddle down the hall to our bedroom. With my trusty bag in one hand and a can of Coke (regular, no diet for me) in the other, I settle into bed to watch my favorite show *The Biggest Loser*, of all things. With a collection of crumbs piling up on my PJs, I wipe my greasy fingers on my pillowcase as I take another swig of cola.

I had become accustomed to following this same repulsive routine of eating every day and night; it had become my comfort food. In fact, if eating was a varsity sport at Forest High, I would have been a letterman. I was in a league of my own and was all-state in the sports of engorgement, gastrointestinal fulfillment, and digestion. My wife was constantly pointing out to me that I ate too quickly and that I needed to slow down and perhaps taste what I had just inhaled. But that wasn't for me; food was to be conquered. I figured that the faster I ate, the more I could eat, with no opportunity for anyone to lick the plate clean before I did. I thought I had the greatest eating plan in the world.

I had a rather unique eating method, in that for the first eighteen hours of the day, I would nearly starve myself. Each morning, I would skip breakfast and, to prepare for the greatest meal of the day, I would also avoid eating lunch. When supper came, I was absolutely ravenous. I would start with two to three servings of whatever Sue was serving that evening, and to top it all off, for dessert, I would eat a whole pie. Not one piece, but the whole pie. I expected my wife to have a pie baked each night for me, and if my daughters wanted a piece of *my* pie, I would tell my wife that she had better bake two, because they were not going to have a piece out of my pie. If my wife did not have a pie ready for me, then I would go to the local supermarket and buy a cheap, processed pie. My favorite was always apple, which I justified by saying that at least I was getting my proper intake of the fruit group.

After suppertime, I would recline on my chair and wait for bedtime, where the eating would begin again. During those few hours on the couch, I would entertain myself with a Coke in my hand, while playing an online card game called Euchre. During those card games, I would find myself obsessing over what flavor of popcorn I would eat as I watched TV before bedtime. The hour before bed was reserved strictly for eating. I would eat for the entire sixty minutes. It was kind of funny, as during those few hours between supper and bedtime, I found that I would develop quite a hunger just waiting for that moment when I could begin eating again.

When the clock in our living room chimed nine, I was like Pavlov's dog, salivating as I was off to the microwave to inhale the sweet smell of buttery popcorn. The smell so engulfed the kitchen that I found myself in a state of nirvana, just as the buzzer went off to signal the start of an hour-long marathon eating orgy. The only problem I had eating popcorn was that I found that, after downing a buttery bag of popcorn, it never fully satisfied my hunger and left me wanting more. So with a bag of cookies in one hand and a bag of potato chips in the other, I found that by the time the lights went out, I was finally full. This was my lifestyle, not for days or weeks, but for years on end. No exaggeration for the effect of this story. These are the facts; the same super-sized routine, the same overstuffed couch, the same pathetic existence, for years on end.

I loved family get-togethers more than anything, as they were a time not for fellowship, but for mass eating. Potlucks were my favorite, where everyone brought their culinary specialty. One Christmas, I vividly remember proudly challenging my family members that I could out-eat each one of them. I was quite surprised when my brother-in-law, a professional body–builder, took up that challenge. At 250 pounds with a rock-solid build, he also loved a good meal, so the contest was on.

A pre-chow-down weigh-in was held before supper, and the family members all gathered around the scale to cheer on their favorite. After the blessing was said, of course, the competition began. Our gastrointestinal onslaught consisted of turkey, stuffing, sweet potatoes, cranberry sauce, and all the trimmings. It was a feast to behold. The best part about our family Christmas dinner was always the desserts afterward, and there was not a doubt in my mind that I would save room for plenty. The competition was fierce during the meal portion, like two heavyweight prizefighters going toe-to-toe. We both went up to fill our plates not twice, not three times, but four times. I was determined not to let my brother-in-law beat me. After all, I had been training for this day for months.

I was surprised to see how he kept up with me, forkful for forkful. Even though I was weighing in at 220 pounds of grade-A flab and back fat, and he tipped the scale at 250 pounds of chiseled physique, he could pack away the food as well. At the moments when I seemed to be slowing down, I told myself, keep going, you can do this. Like in a race, the time to pull away from the rest of the pack is in the last one hundred meters, and with dessert time approaching, I knew I had him right where I wanted him. This was the time when I knew I could pull away from my competitor. With ample experience of eating a whole pie after supper, I was waiting to see the shock on my brother-in-law's face as he went for a single piece of pie, while I went for all eight pieces at once. As we both sat down at the table he glanced over at me and saw that I had taken the entire pie. A look of defeat encompassed his face. The entire family was both amazed and horrified that I had taken the entire pie and left not a piece for anyone else. After all, this was a competition, and there was no room for losers. This was my moment!

As I finished the entire pie, I knew the winner's podium was waiting for me. Had I been able to achieve the impossible? Was I able to beat my brother-in-law in the show down of the year? As my brother-in-law stepped upon the scale he immediately began to feel queasy. As the scale needle moved past his original weight the moment of truth was about to happen; he seemed to turn a never-before-seen shade of grey, as he was about to lose his entire Christmas meal. The needle on the scale wiggled back and forth for a few seconds and then stopped. My brother-in-law had gained 5 pounds, an impressive improvement from only sixty minutes earlier.

Like a champion about to step on the podium, I took one last moment to reflect upon my dietary accomplishment of the past the past hour. Eating was my sport of choice. It was who I had become, and I was not going to let any compilation of biceps, pecs, and six-pack abs take me down. As the needle on the scale began its journey skyward at breakneck speed, I had sensed that this moment would be mine. Then the needle stopped. I had achieved the impossible! I had gained 6 pounds in sixty minutes.

That moment would be forever etched in my mind. The hours that followed that meal would remind me never to do that again. The upset stomach, bloating, and indigestion would haunt me and my wife throughout the night. At the risk of crossing the line into TMI, I spilled more gas than the Exxon Valdez that night. It was something I vowed I would never do again. As I got home that night, I realized that I had turned into something I did not want to become. I had become a food-aholic, and I needed to make a change.

Although I am not a diet expert or professional in the area of weight loss, I knew I had to start losing weight in order to fulfill my dream of running a marathon and qualifying for the Boston Marathon. After that cold December winter's night when I put on my running shoes and ran 5K in the dark, I also knew it was time for me to change my eating habits. To help me in my quest to lose weight, I sought the advice of my brother-in-law, who was not only a weightlifter, but a nutrition fanatic. His plan was simple. Most people eat three square meals a day—breakfast, lunch, and dinner, and this pattern of eating was a way of life for many individuals. But some nutrition experts believe that more frequent meals could be better. Eating six small meals a day, they say, helps regulate blood sugar, control cravings, and keep hunger at bay.

Although there are many experts in the area of weight loss and eating healthy who have varying opinions, I decided to try the "eat every three hours" strategy. I have found, over the past few years since making these changes, that eating six times a day still works best for me. In my quest to become a marathon runner, I noted that a marathon is not about the race, it's about commitment. It's not about instant gratification, it's about endurance. It's not about the thrill, it's about passion. To run a marathon, you need to not only commit to the sport, you need to commit to yourself. To run a marathon, you need to be a runner, and you need to eat healthy and have a proper nutrition balance.

The key to eating healthy is choosing the right foods and eating in moderation throughout the day. This can help you lose weight, while keeping you energized. Hunger is always the enemy of the person who is trying to lose weight. The hunger pain that usually occurs between meals is usually a signal for us to snack on unwholesome foods like chocolate bars, or my former ally, chips. But if you take your total calorie intake per day and divide it into smaller meals throughout the day, hunger will not be a problem.

Calorie requirements are determined by sex, age, physical activity levels, and weight-loss goals. Most adults need between 1,500-2,500 calories for weight loss, unless they are very active. To make the most of each meal, foods like lean meat (chicken), low-fat dairy (yogurt, milk, and cheese), nuts, beans, whole grains, fruits, and vegetables are a good source of protein.

Contrary to my former eating regimen, I learned that skipping the morning meal is a sure way to gain weight. What I have found is that your morning meal provides fuel for your brain, and it is an important meal to fuel your body throughout the day. It replenishes your supply of glucose, after you have gone through the night not eating anything for up to ten hours. Breakfast provides a significant proportion of the day's total nutrient intake, and a good breakfast will help prevent over eating later in the day. A healthy breakfast should consist of a variety of foods. Fruits, whole grain cereal, skim milk, boiled eggs, and oatmeal are examples of a healthy breakfast.

To fuel my body through the day, I have found the secret that each mini-meal should include a blend of protein and fiber-rich complex carbohydrates. Protein and fiber give you the feeling of being satisfied and will keep you from feeling hungry. My mid-morning meal consists of a granola bar, a banana with peanut butter, or a few handfuls of mixed nuts or almonds. Lunch consists of chicken breast, fruits, and vegetables. My mid-afternoon snack is a basic repeat of the mid-morning snack, and dinner usually consists of white meat, vegetables, pasta, and/or sweet potatoes. The evening snack usually consists of yogurt, bananas, or grain cereal. The question that I hear quite often is, "Do you still eat desserts and junk food?" For the most part, the answer is no. However, everything is permissible in moderation.

The key to eating several times a day is moderation: you must control your portions. It would be very easy to fall into the trap of over eating. When I am at a restaurant, I tend to order foods with no sauces, or instead just order a salad. Like running a marathon, eating healthy requires determination, dedication, and perseverance. There are great rewards when you start shifting from high-calorie snacks to balanced mini-meals. There is no definitive data to support either the three-meals-a–day or the six-meals-a-day method as the preferred way to lose weight, and it is therefore about choosing what works for you. If you are the person who has difficulty eating small amounts at a meal, or if you have a hard time stopping once you get started, then eating six times a day may not be for you.

Weight loss ultimately comes down to how much energy (or calories) is consumed, as opposed to how often or how regularly you eat. The rule of thumb for weight maintenance is: calories in, equals calories out. Once you balance nutrition with exercise, you will start to see not only weight loss, but your energy levels through the day will increase. The goal in running the Boston Marathon is like a castle in the air; the foundation of healthy eating and exercise will get me to my dream.

Does this plan work, you may ask yourself? Well, at the risk of using a food metaphor, the proof is in the pudding. In one year, with the combination of exercise and eating every three hours, I lost over 70 pounds. After one year, I started to realize that I was actually beginning to lose too much weight, and my running speed started to decrease, due to a lack of energy. I was outputting more calories than I was taking in. I went from 220 pounds to 140 pounds. I knew this weight could not sustain me in any marathon attempt, so I needed to eat a little more during my six meals a day. Once I achieved balance, I found my ideal weight was around 155 pounds. Not only was I feeling better, but I had set personal bests in all my races. I am now actually winning first place in running races, not in eating contests, and this is where I wanted to be as I approached my first marathon, attempting to qualify for Boston.

MILE 40

THE ROAD OF
DISAPPOINTMENTS

"We must accept finite disappointment, but never lose infinite hope."

—Dr. Martin Luther King Jr.

I had always been told that you cannot start the next chapter of your life if you keep re-reading the last one. So now, with my new pair of running shoes, a new diet, and a new outlook on life I was ready to begin my new chapter in life. I was excited! This was a new year. I always thought it was funny how people became so worked up about what they ate between Christmas and the New Year, when in reality they really should be worried about what they eat between the New Year and Christmas.

I was determined more than ever that, this year, I was going to conquer new territories and climb any mountain that stood in my way. You are never too old to become the star of your own dreams, and I was ready to start on the road to Boston. I knew full well that when you travel on a road, there are potential dangers lurking around corners, and unseen accidents can occur at any time, but I was prepared for anything—or so I thought!

The dark, cold, winter nights of January 2008 would beckon me to stay inside in the comfort of my own home, but this was not going to deter me from reaching my goal. Working long, emotionally challenging days as an educator in an elementary school, coupled with my weight issues, caused me to be dog-tired when I came home from a full day at school. Running was the last thing I wanted to do. After supper, I would hear the couch calling my name, inviting me to sit down and enjoy the comforts of a warm, comfortable chair that was just waiting for a friend to fill its emptiness. As I would prepare for my run each night, I would be continually reminded by my subconscious that running is hard work and requires a great amount of energy, which I often lacked at the end of the day. Like a skier heading out to the slopes, I would bundle myself with every piece of warm clothing I could find. With a 36-inch waist, I found that I could not wear the nice running tights, but instead had to settle for the extra-large woolly jogging pants, the ones with an expandable elastic waist. As I would head out the front door each night, I caught myself asking the same question, "Are you sure you want to do this?"

After three weeks of running, I was becoming discouraged. After each run, I checked myself in for the daily weigh–in, and each night the scale would say the same thing—sorry, no weight loss today, come back tomorrow. I thought I was doing everything right. I was eating right and exercising right, yet I didn't understand why the pounds weren't falling off me. In fact, I was becoming stressed. I was running in the cold, dark, winter nights, eating only what was healthy, and I was not losing any weight. Then it dawned on me. Maybe the only way to get rid of stress was to go back to my old lifestyle, since "stressed" spelled backward is "desserts." If I ate more desserts, I would have less stress, or so my refrigerator told me.

But I was determined to see that scale squeal with joy when those pounds would start falling off. I knew it was only a matter of time. Then it hit me. Mount Everest was waiting right around the bend for me, and I didn't even see it coming. The biggest test of faith, determination, and perseverance was about to be given to me, a test which would change the course for my life and my family's life. This mountain that we were about to climb would challenge the very core of who we were, and it would challenge me as a runner to never give up.

I have a wonderful, close-knit family, and although not perfect, they are very supportive and loving towards each other. I am the oldest of five children; I have three brothers and one sister. My sister is the youngest of the family, and we often thought she was the most spoiled child in our family, but Mom and Dad loved us all the same. Watching my parents proceed through life would teach us that, in order to succeed, we first must believe. The future always belongs to those who believe in the beauty of their dreams. My parents were living proof that, with hard work and determination, you can do anything you set your mind to in life, even those things which seem to be impossible.

When I was thirteen years old, my mother started her own janitorial business. I knew this business was going to be trouble for me. It meant that I was going to have to work, and I had long ago decided that work was not knitted in the fibers of my being. With a mop in one hand and a toilet brush in the other, my way of life was about to change. Cleaning and scrubbing toilets was no way to spend my teen years, but believe it or not, those years would prepare me for my greatest dream: running the Boston Marathon. The countless hours that my mother and father put into this business would teach me that nothing comes easy, and to do the impossible you have to work hard at it. My parents poured their heart and soul into this business, for which I am very grateful. This business would grow from one employee (me), to over one hundred employees in a matter of a few years. It would provide me with the very income I needed to go on to university, purchase my own home, and start my very own family. This business would not only provide money for our family, but it also drew us closer together, as well. It was something we did together; it was something we all had in common. The dream of owning a family business had come true.

This family business experienced several metamorphoses throughout the years before finally blossoming into what it is now, a laundry facility plant. This laundry plant now provides linens for hotels, hospitals, nursing homes, and health care facilities. Over thirty employees were employed at this plant, including my three brothers who would work full-time in the business. My father had retired from a local oil refinery a few years ago and he devoted not only his entire income to see this business grow, but invested his retirement years into this business venture as well. My father was determined to take this business to the next level.

The business was growing and expanding into several different areas in the winter of 2008. Life was good, until disaster struck. One of the greatest challenges a person can face is losing everything they own in one catastrophic swoop. Like Job in the Old Testament who, though a good and righteous man, suffered unbearable tragedies and was tested by Satan to see whether or not he would remain faithful to God even if he lost everything, our family was about to go through a series of tests, unbeknownst to us. The question that remained unanswered was: would we remain true to God?

On Friday, February 15, 2008, our family encountered a heaping helping of disaster washed down with a glass of despair. At around two in morning, my father received a phone call from my brother Shawn, informing my parents that the business and facility was on fire. My father told him that he would be right over, but just before leaving out the door he informed my mother as to what was happening. My mother was very calm upon hearing the news, and shortly after my father arrived at the scene he realized that nothing was going to be left. Our family business of twenty-five years was destroyed by fire.

With a single blow of death, nothing was left standing. Over two million dollars-worth of assets were up in smoke in an instant. To stand there on that day, in the presence of smoke, rubble, and ash, was as if death had left its indelible fingerprint on our business and our lives. As a growing business, we had rather foolishly decided to cut costs by getting minimal insurance on our business. The net loss to the family business would exceed over one million dollars. We never believed in a million years that it would be us who would become victim to such a devastating tragedy. We always thought it would happen to the other guy, but not us.

With very little insurance money coming, our family assumed that the business was done. Feelings of despair, helplessness, confusion and many unanswered questions left us wondering why God had allowed this to happen, especially when things were going so well. We knew that, according to the promise in Romans 8:28, "God causes all things to work together for good to those who love God, to those who are called according to his purpose," but how God was going to do good work through this, we could not see. However, in the midst of the storm, my parents somehow praised God for what He was going to do. This was truly an amazing sight to see. Much like Thomas Edison, that great inventor who at sixty-seven years old saw his factory destroyed by a fire, in his response the next morning, stated, "There's value in disaster. All our mistakes are burned up. Thank God, we can start anew."

One of the blessings we received that night was that no one was hurt or killed in this monstrous fire. The fire had started after midnight, and it took twenty firefighters nearly five hours to contain the fire. They remained there during the next twelve hours, pouring water on the hotspots as the stubborn fire would not die down. By the time the flames were doused, the entire building collapsed from the intense heat. The fire marshal, police, and detectives worked around the clock to determine the cause of this fire, but it was left "undetermined." Like Job, we knew God had allowed this for a reason, and like Job, we found our parents saying, "The Lord giveth, and the Lord hath taken away; blessed be the name of the Lord," (Job 1:27). We knew that it was by God's hand that he had given us this business, and it was His to do with as He wanted to do. Although we may not understand the hand of God, we had to trust Him through the fire. God has never let us down before, and we knew He would not let us down now.

As we watched nearly three decades of blood, sweat, and toil burn, we knew we had a choice to make: either walk away, or somehow find a way to start again. We heard whispers from the community that "it would never start again." Our family did something that we were told was impossible to do: we rallied together to once again prove that *yes, you can* start over and build again!

Standing there in the rubble at three in the morning, my father made a call to my mother to let her know that everything was lost, and asked what would she like to do. Either they could walk away with the little insurance money there would be, or rebuild it for my three brothers who were making a full-time living from the business. With no hesitation at all, my mother's answer was, "You know what you have to do."

God provided all the calmness and wisdom my father needed to work through all of the obstacles thrown at him. My father was also suffering with a head neuralgia issue at the time, which was very debilitating.

There was no doubt in my father's mind that God was going to direct them through it all. Then, amongst all of what was going on that day, my father received a call from another police department in a city miles away that his prodigal son was in jail. (My father would call him the prodigal son, in that he was the only one of the five children who decided he wanted a lifestyle like my father had many years before. As my father would say, "The apple doesn't drop too far from the tree.") The drinking and riotous living had given him a one-way ticket to jail. Instead of tending to the fire on that day, my father chose to devote all of his energy and attention to my brother. The day when he lost everything, he bailed his son out of jail. To my father, family was more important than possessions, and before my father attended to the fire, he took the time to provide some direction for my brother, before moving onto rebuilding our business.

As written in the *London Free Press*, my brother Shawn, the operating manager of our business, was quoted as saying, "We certainly intend to be back, stronger and better than before." While walking through the ruins the next day, my father asked my brother Shawn if there was any money in the building prior to the fire, hoping that everything had been put into the bank, as they were going to need all the money they could get to purchase linen for the following day to provide for their customers. My brother had stated that there was $30,000 cash in the deposit book that was left in the office, something my father did not want to hear. As my father and brother moved through the ashes of what was once the office my father saw what looked like a charred book. As he gave that book a little kick, out popped the $30,000. It was a miracle that only the hand of God could accomplish. God knew exactly what we needed and when we needed it.

Four years later, our family business is back and flourishing like never before, proving once again that nothing is impossible. Today, God has blessed our business, as it is now twice the size it was four years ago, and it continues to grow beyond our wildest imaginations.

As I went for my daily run that weekend, after seeing such devastation, I found myself inspired once again by a father/son team. This time, it was my own father and his sons. To watch my father give praise to God and not once curse Him during one of the darkest hours of his life gave me hope. Although I was not losing any weight, it gave me hope that, as I place my faith and trust in God, He would work out the finer details of seeing the dream through. Although I was not seeing any visible outward changes, I knew deep down that my body had to be changing. I had noticed that my outlook was changing for the good. I was starting to have more energy and was feeling good about myself.

Then it happened again. Round two of despair and disaster was waiting for us just around the next corner. This time, the mountain seemed impenetrable to go through. It was confirmed earlier that my mother, at age sixty-four, had stage two breast cancer, and chemotherapy had just begun for her. The side effects of the chemotherapy had just started to take its vicious toll on her health, when she received the news that her business had just been destroyed by a fire. The blow of death had conquered all she had worked for. It was now final; not only had her health deteriorated, but she had just lost everything she had worked for. I wondered at that time how much a person can take before giving up. Once again, what I didn't realize was that God was giving me a visual example of "Yes, You Can!" *Yes, you can* keep going, even when the storms of life blow in from the sea.

Just a few months before the fire, during a routine doctor's check-up, it was noted that my mother had a heavy mass forming on one of her breasts. The news was not favorable. This diagnosis resulted in two emergency operations for my mother, one to remove the lump, and the second one to remove several lymph nodes that were cancerous. During this trying time, my mother continued to persevere through the pain and tragic news that this cancer could take her life. I was amazed that her faith in the Lord remained unshaken. Her joy was always evident whenever we would visit her. She had placed her faith and trust in the Lord. She knew where she was going, if God decided to take her home. My mother constantly reminded me that even the longest human life is merely a single grain of sand on the infinite beach of the eternal life to come.

As I watched my mother fight the side-effects of chemo, I stood amazed at her determination, perseverance, and willingness to stay the course. Her hair was now starting to fall out. She had a loss of appetite. She suffered nausea, vomiting, diarrhea, and insomnia, just to name a few of the side-effects my mother was experiencing through this storm, but she remained optimistic about the future.

My mother was a fighter, and all through the chemo, even while losing everything she had worked for in her business, she was the anchor on the ship our family sailed. Her optimistic attitude would become my driving force to achieving my dream. The news was given days after the fire that my mother would require thirty treatments of radiation after her chemo. Like chemotherapy, radiation therapy has many side effects. This treatment would destroy any cancer cells that may stick around after surgery, however, it would come with more side-effects and more pain. My mother remained undeterred and would not stray from her course. She often reminded us that, after the rain there's a rainbow, after a storm there's calm, after the night there's a morning, and after an ending there's a new beginning. She knew that new beginnings are worth fighting for!

This was exactly the encouragement I needed to see and hear from both my mother and father. I have always said, "More is caught than taught," and by their example it proved to me, "Yes, I can" do the impossible. It is often said, "What doesn't kill you makes you stronger," and this adage has been proven by my parents. My mother would learn, months later, that she had won the battle with cancer. She had become victorious in her fight for her life. My father continued to not only be by her side, but fought hard at rebuilding the business they once had. Regardless of unseen obstacles ahead, they never lost hope. They believed that a new day would come, and when that new day comes, another dream will be born.

What I didn't know was that God was preparing me for my greatest challenge that was awaiting me on the road ahead. This challenge would rock my very existence, and once again, I would question why God had given me this dream to run a marathon, when He knew this mountain was coming. It was my turn to face the giants in the barren land that lay in wait for me.

MILE 50

THE MOUNTAINS ARE COMING

"... but those who hope in the Lord will renew their strength. They will soar on wings like eagles; they will run and not grow weary, they will walk and not be faint."

—*Isaiah 40:31*

Spring was in the air, and the robins were announcing the return of the warm weather. The cold Canadian days were getting longer and dominated by sunshine, and the winter running clothes were slowly being peeled off, layer by layer. It was just days before the official start of a new season, and winter running was finally coming to an end. I found that winter running could be very unpleasant and daunting; slippery sidewalks, cold hands, frozen toes, dropping temperatures, wind chill, and even overdressing can make any run uncomfortable. I found myself battling my inner spirit each day that was intent on telling me to stay home and enjoy the warmth of my living room, as opposed to experiencing yet another sub-zero Sarnia evening.

As the saying goes, "It takes four weeks for you to see your body changing. It takes eight weeks for friends and family to see it, and it takes twelve weeks for the rest of the world." It had now been ten weeks of solid training, and I was still battling stage one and waiting to see the changes within me. I had been running consistently each night, determined to win the battle with my weight and wondering when that magical day would come that would signal the descent down the scale. Then it happened!

I had just returned home from a two week missionary trip to Honduras, when I stepped on the scale and was instantly introduced to the new me. While in Honduras, I could not find a single scale anywhere. It was as if they were non-existent in that country. During those two weeks, I experienced withdrawal symptoms of not stepping on the podium each morning for my daily dose of discouragement, of no weight loss. Those two weeks away seemed like an eternity, and I could hardly wait until I got back home to see if, by the grace of God, I had finally stepped from my plateau. I felt better than ever physically and emotionally, and the meals of rice and beans that served as a staple in Honduras seemed to agree with my diet. I was amazed at how many different ways a country could serve rice and still make it taste good. During this two-week change in diet, it seemed that my pants were getting a bit loose around the waist line, and my shirts were starting to look a little bulky. The moment of truth would soon be revealed.

As I stepped in the front door of my home after returning from Honduras, I was on a new mission. I was like a crazed madman in search of my scale. Deep down, I knew I must have lost some weight, and I wanted to see the results firsthand. My family would have to wait for a few moments to hear the stories of my experiences in Central America, as I needed to greet my long lost friend, my scale. In a look of surprise, I raced by my wife and girls and went downstairs to greet my friend. I knew it had been waiting patiently for me during my absence, and here I was. As I stepped on the podium, the needle did not jump up with lightning speed as it did in the past. In fact, this time it was different. With my heart racing like a Porsche, I watched the needle begin its ascent to an unknown destination. Like a Cadillac on a Sunday afternoon drive, the needle moved with such smoothness, such finesse and grace. The moment of truth was finally revealed. With a holler of excitement, I had done the impossible: I had lost 10 pounds. I had finally lost some weight, and I was feeling more alive than I'd felt in years.

It had been almost twelve weeks of non-stop training, but to see that scale finally concede told me that the long hard nights of training had finally paid off. What an incredible feeling. Like hips, scales don't tell lies, and I could tell by my hips that victory was mine. A belt would not do for my pants, anymore. I now needed new clothes, and for good reason. My family was now looking at the new me. It was the greatest feeling in the world.

As I walked back into my classroom after returning from Honduras, one of my students looked at me and said, "Mr. Harding, are you losing weight?" That statement was music to my ears.

I so longed to hear those words spoken that I meekly and coyly responded, "Why, does it show?"

"Oh, yes, does it ever," was her reply.

Not only had she noticed, but there was a quiet whisper travelling around the school that I had started to lose some fat. These whispers motivated me to lose even more weight. I could hardly wait to show everyone that this was only the beginning. They hadn't seen anything yet. *Just wait*, I thought, *I will show them that all things are possible.*

Not only was my weight decreasing, but my run times were improving as well. I was getting faster. No longer did I have to run at night. I was now a runner. It was in my blood. With a new outlook on life, I marched back into that same store I was in just months ago to buy my first pair of running shoes. This time I was not going to leave empty-handed. This time, I was not going to let anyone deter me from my dream. Not even a well-respected marathoner could discourage me now. I looked for the same saleslady who served me before, but she was nowhere to be found. This time, I had a new saleslady, and with her guidance, I bought my first official pair of running shoes. She then encouraged me to sign up for a road race that was taking place in our community in just three months. It was a 10-kilometer race that would start in Port Huron, Michigan, cross over the Blue Water International Bridge, and finish in Sarnia, Ontario, Canada. I had never even considered running a race before, and for good reason. I was never a runner.

But things were different now, and running was my passion. To start running marathons, I would need to start running races. A 10-kilometer race seemed daunting at first, especially when I had never run that far in my life. I was accustomed to running only 5 kilometers a night, and that was running only against me, not against legitimate competition. I knew though that, if wanted to run the Boston Marathon, I would need to change my running habits. This race was held in June, and I had two and a half months to train for it. It could be done! So I signed up.

It was now official, I had signed up for my first road–race, and I was more than excited. It was my first real *SMART* goal in the competitive world of running. *SMART* is an acronym for Specific: a 10-kilometers road race. It was Measureable: I could accomplish this. It was Attainable: after all, I could run 5 kilometers. It was Realistic: I was both willing and able to work toward this distance. It was Timely: the race was two and a half months away. This was the perfect motivation I needed to expand my running horizons. In fact, if I could achieve this goal of running 10 kilometers then I would be one-fourth of the way to running a marathon, and that thought gave me hope that I would actually really be running marathons.

Each day for the next two months, I would go out and run to one more hydro pole than the run before. I was determined to give it my best shot. After two and a half months of training, my running debut had come. I was a little nervous doing a 10-kilometer run, especially when I had only run a long run of 8 kilometers before this. The telephone pole method did not exactly meet the mark, but in truth, that didn't matter. This race, I was going to make my own personal running history, as it was time for me to make my entrance in the world of competitive racing. I knew that only those who would risk going too far could possibly find out how far one could go. I knew 10 kilometers was not too far, and it was within my reach.

It was June 2008, and race day was here. I had lost a pretty sizeable portion of the spare tire I once wore around my waist, and I was 20 pounds lighter than I was six months ago. As a newbie to running, I did everything according to the experts' advice. I picked up my race packet early, I chose my pre-race breakfast wisely, I arrived at the starting line over an hour early, and I even started the race near the front of the pack. With over five hundred runners starting the race, I was pumped. After all, I was now a runner, and I was aiming to finish with a great time.

As I stood at the starting line, I could see the Blue Water Bridge in the background. The middle of the span of the bridge marked the half-way point of the race. At that moment, a nervous feeling came over me as I looked at the height and stature of this massive bridge. It was impressive. With a total length of just over 1 kilometer and a height of 233 feet, I suddenly had a feeling of despair in my gut. This mountain seemed intimidating, almost telling us runners that the end of the race would be at its peak. I was reminded once again, at that moment, that the best way to climb a mountain was one step at a time. And so the race began.

As the gun was fired, a surge of adrenalin flowed through my veins giving me the incredible feeling of running with the wind. As I crossed the first kilometer marker, I immediately remarked to my inner self that this was easy. That was until I came to the bridge. The on-ramp to the bridge was the warm up to the bridge itself, and I was feeling the effects of pain, tiredness, and being overwhelmed by the sheer height of the bridge. As I began the ascent up the bridge, I could hear the iron girders laughing as the wind howled between the trusses that held it in place.

This laugh seemed to taunt me by saying this was not possible, quit, give up, you can't do this. Then at that moment the words by Dick and Rick Hoyt entered my mind and said, *Yes, you can!*

That was the little bit of motivation I needed, because I knew I had worked too hard to quit at this time and place. I continued to push myself to the top of this mountain, and as I neared the peak, I looked out over Lake Huron to see an ocean liner passing underneath the bridge. This freighter looked so small as I towered well above it; it felt that I was soaring on the wings of eagles. I was now halfway finished with the race, and the weariness seemed to disappear from my body as the descent down the bridge began. Like in eating, the time to pull away from the pack was during the dessert time, and this was now the icing on the cake. It was time to leave everything I had on the road.

I ran like never before, and as I approached the 9-kilometer mark, I knew running was in my blood. I could hear the crowd cheering as I approached the finish line in Canatara Park. And there it was; the end was in sight. I sprinted the last 500 meters, passing several runners along the way. An exhilarating feeling of freedom came over me as I crossed the finished line. I had done it!

There, cheering and waiting for me as I crossed that finish line, was my family, my cheerleaders. With their cameras in hand and smiling faces, the overwhelming look of pride engulfed their faces as if to say, "This is my dad, and he is going to run the Boston Marathon one day." I quickly glanced down at my watch to see what my time was, and to my amazement I had run that race in a time of 45:22, a time that I thought was incredible, despite the fact that I was still carrying a whole lot of extra weight that I could ultimately get rid of to make me run even faster. I made my way over to see the race results that were being posted nearby. I could hardly contain myself as I read my name on the finishers list. I had placed 63rd out of 466 finishers. With my first medal around my neck, I ran back to my family to tell them the good news; the good news that life would be different now. I was now a runner, and this was just the beginning of a whole new way of life. That afternoon I went home and, in my excitement, I signed up for another 10-kilometer race that was happening in October in Niagara Falls, Ontario. I had four months to train hard and to prove once again, *yes, you can* improve in your running ability.

The following week, I was determined to run faster than ever before, and then yet another challenge hit me. As I went out for a run that week, disaster struck. Severe pains were shooting up and down my leg. Something was wrong; something was not right. I limped home the rest of the way, and I found myself to be in excruciating pain. I had never known this type of pain before, and I knew I had done some sort of damage to my leg. I justified my pain by saying, "No pain, no gain," but I knew this pain was not going away. The days that followed continued to bring the same results: pain, swelling, and soreness. I could hardly stand on my leg, and I needed to seek professional help. I knew that injuries could sideline athletes, sometimes even indefinitely, and I did not want to see this quest come to an end. So with the advice of some friends, I went and sought out a physiotherapist.

Having never been to a physiotherapist before, I wasn't sure what to expect. Maybe a few pills and some rest would be the order of the day, but unfortunately, that wasn't the news that I got. Because of the lack of knowledge I had in the sport of running, and not being on a proper running program, I had been diagnosed with *iliotibial band syndrome* (ITBS). In my ignorance, this term sounded Greek to me, and I had no idea if that meant my running days were over, or not. My heart began to knock through my chest as if to say, "Pay attention to what you are about to hear. It will save your dream." I was all ears as my physiotherapist explained to me that ITBS is one of the leading causes of lateral knee pain in runners. I learned that this band extends from the outside of the pelvis, over the hip and knee, and inserts just below the knee. The iliotibial band is crucial to stabilizing the knee during running. The pain may not occur immediately while running, but may intensify over time, especially as the foot strikes the ground. As the physiotherapist continued to explain what was happening with my knee, I found my mind wandering as I pondered how I would run this next race, when I couldn't even walk out the front door without my knee throbbing in pain.

The good news was I now knew what the problem was, and that was half the solution to fixing the problem. My doctor explained that, with rest, ice, stretching, and therapy, I could overcome this obstacle, too. Then I heard the word "needle." Needles and I do not go agree with each other, and I could not see how a needle would help in this instance. What I soon learned that it was not one needle that I would receive, but a whole series of needles. This type of treatment was called "dry needling."

I read the following about dry needling: "Dry needling targets trigger points, which are the direct and palpable source of pain. Dry needling is an invasive procedure in which a filiform needle is inserted into the skin and muscle directly at a myofascial trigger point. A myofascial trigger point consists of multiple contraction knots, which are related to the production and maintenance of the pain cycle. Each trigger point will elicit a local twitch response and is used to improve the overall outcome of the pain." The only question I had after this explanation was, "Could I start running sooner, if I tolerated this procedure?" The response was yes, with dry needling, therapy, and ice, I would be on the road running sooner than later. That is all I needed to hear. "Sign me up," I said. I wanted to begin immediately.

It just so happened that my physiotherapist was certified in the art of "dry needling." Was this the hand of God upon me that I could be so blessed to have the one and only physiotherapist in the entire region right in front of me certified in this form of treatment? And what I didn't even know was this same physiotherapist even attended the same church as I did. How could this be? Even though I attended the largest church in our community, I didn't even realize that God had blessed me once again by connecting me with just the right person and solution for me.

I must admit that I was a little apprehensive receiving the dry needling treatment. What if something went wrong? What if my physiotherapist hit the wrong point? Could more harm be done than good? The real question I had to ask myself was, "Did I trust this person?" Although I did not know her personally, I would have to go on her experience and the success stories of people who had experienced this type of treatment before. If I could answer this question with a "yes," then nothing was stopping me.

And "yes," it was. After experiencing the first of several dry needling treatments, I had no idea that the feeling of pain was a good feeling. The twitch responses in my muscles were painful, but it was an amazing release of tension as the pain would subside. It would be a matter of a few weeks when I would be out running again. To help aid me in my running I would have to wear an IT compression band wrapped around my knee. This brace would stabilize my knee for months, as I continued to run toward my dream. Not only was my leg feeling much better, but my physiotherapist, also a runner, gave me something I was not expecting. She gave me some advice. Although it was quite simple, it was most effective. She simply said, "Don't run every day, but instead try running every other day, and only go 10-percent further in mileage than the week before." This plan would propel me into my next race.

As the summer was drawing to a close, and the fall colors were starting display themselves on the trees, running was at an all-time high for me. I was once again feeling alive and running like the wind. It was race time again, and this time I knew I was even more ready. The pain in my leg had disappeared, and I had continued to lose more weight. I was now down over 40 pounds since January, and 20 pounds lighter than my last 10-kilometer race in June. I was in the best shape of my life and living the dream.

So with my family in tow and cameras in hand, we headed off to the Niagara Falls International 10-kilometer race. My home-grown paparazzi were ready to capture this event for years to come. This was our first official race where we journeyed away from our home city and our first holiday as a family for many years. With four teenage girls, our family is always lively, cheerful, and excessively loud, especially on the sidelines in races. Just the way I like it. They are the driving force for me to do well and to fight the good fight. Like the apostle Paul in the New Testament, I always say to my girls, "Fight the good fight, finish the race and keep the faith," (2 Timothy 4:7), and today I was going to finish the race like never before. I was intent on coming home with a first place ribbon!

As I approached the starting line, I did something that was somewhat uncharacteristic of me. I started right on the starting line. I thought, since I was now a runner and I was a good runner, *Why can't I start with the elite runners? After all, I will become one of them one day.* As my foot touched the starting line, I looked up and saw the birds flying overhead and was reminded once again that I would soar on wings like eagles. Today was my day!

The sound of the gun to start the race was a sweet sound, and I ran that day with all of my heart and soul. I found myself running as if God Himself was running right beside me. As I looked at the palette of beautiful fall colors all around me, I was reminded that not only, "Yes, You Can" but "Yes, you are doing it." As I rounded the 5-kilometer marker, I was doing it. I was in the top ten runners of the race! As I passed the runners on my way back, I could hear them saying through their smiles and nods of approval, "That's a good runner." The end was now in sight. I could hear the roaring falls rushing over the cliffs. I knew those falls would be deafened by my daughter's screaming cheers as I came within sight.

There it was—the end was in sight. I could feel the thunderous roar energize my last sprint to the finish! As I crossed over the finishing line, I could hear the announcer say over the loud speakers, "And this is Wes Harding from Sarnia, Ontario. He is our first-place winner in the men's age 40-44 category." With a time of 42:59, I had come in 9th overall and first place in my age category. Once again, the impossible had been accomplished.

There was no greater feeling than seeing my family after that race. Their words of encouragement and hugs proved that I was on the road to becoming a very competitive runner. We would soon be doing more travelling to other races and discovering the world together as a team. "Get ready," I told my girls. "Boston is coming!"

What I didn't know was a mountain the size of Mount Everest was waiting for me around the corner, and I didn't even see it coming. This obstacle would be my greatest challenge to overcome. It would not only shake up my world but it was going to change the way I lived, as I heard the doctor say to me . . .

"You had a heart attack!"

MILE 60

THE BIGGEST MOUNTAIN YET

"When you are going through something hard and wonder where God is, remember the teacher is always quiet during a test. Trust in the Lord"

"I hate tests," lamented one of my seventh-grade students right before I was about to hand him his math test, "and why do you have to give them to us?"

"But tests are good for you," I explained, trying to console him. "Tests determine not only what you have learned, but what to do next."

"I still hate them," he said with a smile, knowing full well that this was an argument he was not going to win.

Little did I realize that prophetic statement would be the very same answer that God would give me when I asked Him why He allowed testing to come into my own life, as well. I didn't realize it at the time, but like my student, God was preparing me for the biggest test of my life. What I didn't know was how I was going to perform on this test. I had, in fact, been prepped for this moment, and I didn't even realize it. The timing of this test that God would give would be like a pop quiz that a teacher usually gives his students, unexpected and unannounced. The difference being that this pop quiz had serious repercussions if I failed. This test only had one question on it, and that was, "Did I really trust God?" And God was silent.

Things were going well for me up to that point. After finishing first place in my age category in the 10K race in Niagara Falls, I was preparing to train through the winter again. Although not my favorite time of year to train, it had to be done. Early mornings, sore legs, painful cramps, and long hours of training in the sub-Arctic winds that blow off of Lake Huron would need to be put in, if I wanted to qualify for Boston. In short, I would have to work hard to achieve this level of running.

All through my teen years, *work* was literally a dirty, four-letter word, but I was accustomed to getting dirty, and that suited me fine. There were great rewards to be had when you got down on your hands and knees to scrub toilets. Using your muscles and willpower, with the reward being the satisfaction of completing a job well done. I knew I didn't need to impress anyone other than myself, and I didn't want my thoughts to haunt me with the words, "I could have done better, if I tried harder." Even though I hated winter training, I heard the soft, yet powerful voice of Muhammad Ali, that great heavyweight champion of the world saying, "Don't quit. Suffer now, and live the rest of your life as a champion," and a champion I wanted to be. So, I said to myself, "Bring on the crisp, cold Canadian winter!"

For the four months after my bout with that first injury, I had joined a local gym called Ironworks. I had never been to a gym before and for good reason. All my previous weight training came from lifting two liter bottles of pop and bags of cookies. I knew I had to strengthen not only my legs, but also my core mid-section, if I wanted to run a marathon, and the gym was the best place to do this. My physiotherapist had encouraged me to start weight training, since long-distance runners needed a strong core to keep their legs in alignment, especially when the training got long and hard. Besides, I wanted to trade in my six pack of cola for a six pack of muscle: the abs of steel look.

I was a little intimidated when I walked in this gym for the first time, knowing there would be some pretty strong "Ironmen" working out, and with my flabby skin hanging out all over the place, I would be quite a sight. This gym had been recommended to me by my brother-in-law, the professional body-builder, who had eaten my dust during our previous "Battle of the Bulge." He told me that this gym had an exceptional variety of exercise options, including cardio, conditioning, and circuit training, which suited me well, but they also had weights, both freestanding and machine weights, and that is exactly what I needed.

As I walked into that gym, I was amazed by what I saw. The first person to welcome me was the owner, Cam Davies, who not only welcomed me, but personally gave me a tour of what I could expect. As we approached the weight room, I was amazed at the age range that was represented working out. I glanced to my right and saw the most amazing sight. A woman who appeared to be in her sixties was lifting weights. I was surprised to learn from Cam that age sixty was seen long ago in her rearview mirror, as she was actually ninety years old. The years of training had served her well, and she looked extremely fit. I wanted the same for my life. No longer was I intimidated by walking into this gym. Each time I would go to work out, Cam would encourage me to keep going and reminded me that I could fulfill my dreams with hard work. What I didn't know at the time was this weight training would save my life, my running career, and my dream.

As the one-year anniversary of my new lifestyle was approaching, I stepped on the scales to see what a difference a year could make. I had now lost 60 pounds, I was feeling really good about myself, and I was starting to get faster. I felt unstoppable.

In order for me to remain motivated, I had to continually set new goals, so right after Christmas, I set my sights on running a half-marathon (13.1 miles), in the spring of 2009. For Christmas, I purchased a new training book called *Run Less, Run Faster*. This book's title caught my eye, because I wanted to run faster, but I didn't want to be running every day. I was intrigued that the research from this book came from the Furman Institute of Running and Scientific Training (FIRST). It was the very training book I wanted. Its training program limited overtraining and burnout, while producing faster race times, and that was exactly what I needed. It included training plans for novice runners, as well as plans tailored to the new qualifying times for the Boston Marathon, and I bought anything that had the Boston Marathon in it. Like a camel at a water hole, I drank it all in, and soon I found myself enjoying running more than ever.

During the winter months, the training went like clockwork, and once again, spring was in the air. The Boston Marathon was getting ready to be run, and so was my first half-marathon race. As I tuned in on Patriots Day to watch the Boston Marathon begin, my heart leaped for joy. Watching along with the thousands of runners and a half million spectators who lined the route from Hopkinton to Copley Square, I found myself glued to the TV, taking in the sights and the sounds of the marathon. It was almost as if I had been right there running with the elite runners, and then I saw them: Dick and Rick Hoyt. As I watched these two individuals run the race, I heard the announcer say that they had formed a special team of runners called Team Hoyt, who were also running in this marathon. This team consisted of runners from all over the country who were selected by the Hoyts themselves. Consisting of twenty runners, this team would represent Team Hoyt in the marathon and would raise money for the Hoyt Foundation.

I remember commenting to myself at that moment that I wanted to run the Boston Marathon as a qualified runner, and that I wanted to be a part of this amazing team when I did, for it was the Hoyts who inspired me. That "Yes, I can" mantra changed my lifestyle for the good. And so the seed to run with Team Hoyt was planted on that day.

Although I knew there would be many obstacles to overcome (like how to get selected to run with Team Hoyt and meeting the strict qualifying times demanded by the Boston Athletic Association), that did matter. I knew my destiny, and it did not matter what people thought of my dreams. I was going to succeed, and no obstacle would get in my way. In fact, I was not even seeing these as obstacles any more. I was seeing them as opportunities. I always believed that obstacles are things a person sees when he takes his eyes off the goal, and this time I was not going to take my eyes off the goal.

My half-marathon debut had now come. I had been preparing for this day for months, and I was ready. It was Mothers' Day, and what better way to spend Mothers' Day than by standing in the freezing cold for what seemed like an eternity. It was snowing on that morning, and it was now the second week in May. My wife and daughters were bundled up like snowmen as they waited patiently for me to cross the finishing line. I am always amazed at what great lengths my family would go for me, and this meant everything to me. They, too, believed that this dream of running the greatest marathon in the world would actually happen. They've witnessed me when I put my mind to something, and whether it is winning an eating competition, polishing off a bag of chips, or reaching my goal of competing in the Boston Marathon, they know I won't be denied.

As I approached the finish line, I immediately scanned the crowd, searching for my screaming girls. They were my cheering squad and had become my good luck charms. And there they were, with cameras flashing, like I was walking the red carpet. They welcomed me back with open arms after a cold, but successful, 13.1 miles. I was ecstatic! I had finished my first half-marathon. Although there were moments during this race that I wanted to give up, I would continually be reminded that yes, I can do this. With a finishing time of 1:32:00, I had finished thirtieth overall, out of over seven hundred finishers. The marathon distance was next…or so I thought.

It is funny how God allows circumstances and situations to come into our life to get our attention. Sometimes life is going by so fast that He needs us to step off the bus and look around for a moment to appreciate the things we have. I was on a mission, and there was nothing stopping me, that was, until God stepped in. He had different plans for my immediate future, and I didn't even know it was coming.

After driving home after the race, I thought I had the most brilliant of ideas. I signed up for not one road race that afternoon, but two of them. Life was fast-paced now, and road races were becoming a part of my lifestyle. I needed the thrill of the competition to keep me motivated, and I wanted to keep getting faster.

The first race I signed up for was for my first full marathon of 26.2 miles. A feeling of accomplishment came over me as I clicked "confirm" on the website stating that I was now in the marathon. I knew my dream of running a marathon was within reach. This race would be run in Toronto, Ontario, with thousands of runners, and I just knew that I would be qualifying for the Boston Marathon in this race. The second race I signed up for was an afterthought. The Blue Water Bridge International 10-kilometer race was just a few weeks away, and I wanted to prove to myself that I could run this race faster and better than the year before. This time it would be easier. I knew the course, and I knew the competition. I sensed that I could come in the top ten in this race, after coming in 63rd last year in my first 10K ever.

I had heard that the organizers of this race allowed individuals to run this race as a team, and I thought I could put together a "dream team" of runners. This team, I believed, would set new records and do what seemed impossible—eat all the other teams. In my selection of team members, I chose nothing but the best. I choose fast quality runners, two of which had run marathons before. This was going to be the best race ever and, to prove it, I set a nearly impossible goal for myself: I wanted to come in the top ten of all runners. After all, I had now been running for a year and a half.

In order to place in the top ten I needed to run the race in a time of under 40 minutes. Running at this pace would challenge me both physically and mentally, but I knew I could do it. As the great NFL football coach, Jimmy Johnson of the Dallas Cowboys, once said after winning the Super Bowl championship in 1992 and 1993, "The difference between ordinary and extraordinary is that little extra." I was willing to put in that little extra to make this an extraordinary race.

There was a lot of excitement in the air on that Sunday morning in June. Race officials were roaming about, and the YMCA Blue Water Bridge 10K race was about to begin. The summer breezes were blowing ever so lightly, and the temperature was nearing 75 Fahrenheit. There was a light sprinkle of rain that seemed to make the asphalt sizzle as the droplets fell around us. Although overcast, I could see the sun trying to push away the clouds. As I made my way to the front of the starting line, I turned on my iPod to get energized before the starting gun sounded.

As the light drizzle fell around us, I found it ironic that the song that was playing was entitled "I Will Praise You Through the Storm" by Casting Crowns. *There would be no storm today*, I thought, *but like every day of my life, there would be ample praise*. I put my sunglasses on in anticipation of a warm sun coming out. My personal best was going to be set, and what better race to do it in than one in your own hometown. The bridge no longer screamed, "You can't do this," but rather was inviting me to enjoy its scenic view from the top. I was ready for anything, or so I thought.

As the gun sounded, I felt the wind at my back as the warm sun was just starting to peer through the clouds. It seemed like I was flying. Having lost over 70 pounds since my quest for health and fitness had begun, I was indeed free at last. As light as a feather, my race speed after the first kilometer amazed me. I was on track to do even better than I thought. With only a few runners ahead of me, the chase was on.

As I approached the midway point of the race, I couldn't help but be reminded of the beautiful view the bridge so graciously offered. After a moment of reflection, I zoned back in and ran for the finish line. The weather was now considerably warmer, and my body was yearning for a taste of water. As the 6-kilometer water station approached, I glanced over to see a runner pass me. Being as competitive as I am, I was determined not to let him beat me at this point, and I saw my opportunity to overtake him when he paused to get water from the water station. I knew that this was my moment. I flew right past the water station, leaving that runner lagging behind me. Every second counted, and I didn't want anything to slow me down.

As I approached the last kilometer, I could once again hear the crowd. I knew I was in the top ten, and I was going to do the impossible—I was going to set my personal best in a time under 40 minutes. However, something seemed strange within my body. Something I never felt before. It felt as if I was slowing down. I was doing everything possible to keep my legs moving, yet two runners then passed me. What was happening?

As I rounded the corner to the entrance to the park, with only 800 meters to run, I felt an incredible pain shoot up and down the side of my leg. I could barely stand on it. It was as if I had broken my leg. Seconds later, my leg had no feeling in it, but that didn't matter, because I could see the finish line. The end was in sight.

And then it happened! With only four hundred meters to the finishing line, I blacked out and fell, tumbling in a heap onto the warm asphalt.

I remember coming to—who knows how long later—and hearing voices all around me. As I tried to get up, I felt an incredible surge of pain go through me and a voice telling me to stay there. I glanced to my right and saw two individuals on their knees tending to me. I told them, "I have to finish the race first." Besides, I didn't want to let my teammates down. I knew I didn't come to start the race, I came to finish it, and finishing it, I would do. To their amazement, I mustered all my strength and willpower and started running for the finish line. I knew something was definitely wrong; I could hardly bend my legs, and my head hurt. My body was telling me *no more running*, but I would not listen.

As I approached the finish line, my wife and family did not even recognize me. Not only did I look different, but something was horribly wrong. As I crossed over the finish line, my family immediately came over to me with a look of horror on their faces. I could tell by their look that I was not in good shape, at all. I was then greeted by two paramedics who had run across the field to meet me. They sat me down and took my vitals. Something was definitely wrong, and I knew it. But that didn't matter to me. My first question to the paramedics was, "How was my time?" Their silence seemed to indicate that they had something else on their mind quite a bit more critical than my time.

Their next words captured my attention when they said, "We need to get you to the hospital, and we need to get you there immediately." The storm of life had begun.

I had never ridden in an ambulance before. There was no waiting at red lights, and I was intrigued at the notion that the paramedics looked like they were in a panic. *Never mind me,* I thought as I looked at them. They were the ones not looking well. I remember asking the paramedic in the back of the ambulance how I was doing, and in a look of fright she said, "You are not doing well. We need to get you to a doctor, now." That thought scared me to no end, and I immediately stopped taking things so lightly. I knew something was horribly wrong, and I could not believe that this was happening, especially when things were going so well. *Why now, God?* I screamed within me. *Why now?* And God was silent.

As the ambulance arrived at the hospital, I was treated like some kind of royalty. I had the nurses' immediate attention. As they wheeled me past the waiting room, I felt bad for all those patients waiting patiently to see the doctor as I got a "front of the line" ticket to see the doctor. To my amazement, I not only had one doctor, but three came to my attention immediately. It seemed as if I was the star of the show, except this show was not the one I wanted to be in. A look of urgency came over the doctors faces as I was immediately hooked up to more monitors than a TV store had televisions. Wires attached to me were shooting out in every direction. I knew this was not good. I knew this was serious. As the nurse looked at me, she said those very words that would haunt me for days to come, "I think your running days are over."

In my retaliation, I shouted back as the nurse walked out of the room, "That can't be, I am going to run the Boston Marathon one day."

I was in total denial as the nurse turned as she walked out the door. "We will see what the doctor says," she said.

In the silence of my room, I pondered those death-delivering words. What was even worse was, I could not feel the presence of God anywhere. *Where is He?* I thought. *How could he allow this to happen, especially when He brought me this far, only to leave me?* I was living a nightmare, and I wanted the movie to end now.

It would only be a few moments, before I would see my wife's face appear as she walked into my room. The peace that she bought with her seemed to say everything will be alright. As the nurse walked back into the room, an IV bag was administered to me. I looked at the nurse and told her that I had to get going. I had to be at church, because I was speaking in the morning service. I had no time to be waiting around a hospital room. Once again, this nurse would set me straight as she said, "You are not going anywhere, young man. You are staying here."

In my church service later that Sunday morning, an announcement was made from the pulpit that stated I had collapsed in the road race and was rushed to the hospital. A quiet hush filled the audience. My parents were in attendance that morning to hear me speak, and they were totally unaware of the events that had just unfolded. The news left them visibly shaken, as they could not imagine that it was their son who had collapsed in this race. They immediately got up and left the church to be by my side at the hospital. As I was sitting in my room, now alone, I immediately sensed a presence standing over me. It was my parents.

Upon their arrival to the hospital, my mom and dad were immediately ushered to my room. The hospital was in a buzz that a young runner had collapsed, and there was a whisper of uncertainty for this runner.

My father soon left the room to find my wife, who had left to fill out some paper work. My mother was there by my bedside when the emergency room doctor came in to deliver the final blow to my running career. You could hear a pin drop when he said, "You've had a heart attack."

Without batting an eyelid, I responded by saying, "But I didn't have any chest pains."

The doctor then looked at me and in his serious voice said, "We can't prove it just yet, but your heart is sending out a cardiac enzyme that is telling us that there is serious muscle damage that has been done, and we believe it to be your heart. We will know more in the next few days, as we conduct some more extensive tests on your heart. You are staying here, now. There will be no more running for you, now."

The room was now empty, as my mother left to find my wife. As the doctor closed the door behind him, I was left alone again. *Where is God in all this?* I thought. It seemed that not even His presence was in the room. I was all alone with the death of a dream. Then I heard it within me, it was that small, still voice that said, "Do you trust God?"

"God, I hate tests. Why do I have to take this test?" I shouted at the blank walls. And all was quiet as the rain pounded the window of my room.

It was time to go through the storm of life.

MILE 70

LIFE LESSONS LEARNED FROM MY PARENTS

"Life is a shipwreck but we must not forget to sing in the lifeboats."

-Voltaire

Why do bad things happen to good people? I thought to myself. But I already knew the answer. God had a plan, and I just couldn't see what that plan was from my vantage point. In the quietness of that hospital room, I knew full well that God had allowed this collapse to happen for a reason. Nothing escapes God's watchful eye, and nothing takes Him by surprise. God was testing me to see if I would trust Him through this trial.

"Somebody was watching out for you. You are a lucky man," the nurse said to me as she walked into my room and administered the second bag of IV fluids. "You are severely dehydrated," she said, as she placed some warm blankets on my bed. I was too preoccupied with my thoughts to even respond to her.

As she left the room, I was drawn back to the words of "I Will Praise

You Through the Storm," that first song I heard on my MP3 player as the race was about to begin.

"I will praise You in this, Lord," I said, "even though I don't understand why You have allowed this, but I will praise You in this storm." God had never let me down before, and I knew He wasn't about to begin now. As I pondered the words of this song, my mind wandered back to the time when I was a young boy of eight years old, when I asked Jesus to be my forever friend. This moment would be etched in my mind forever. I remembered my mother and I getting down on our knees in my bedroom and talking to Jesus. It was in that moment I had dedicated my life to Him. Although I had no idea what that entailed at such a young age, I did know that, after watching both my mother and father radically change their lives after they accepted Him, I wanted the same for mine. My parents trusted in God, and by their example, they proved to me that God is faithful no matter what happens in life. This would be proven time and time again as they went through the various storms in their own lives, both as individuals and as a couple. I knew that I was not saved by my parents' faith; I knew I had to take ownership of my own faith and ask God into my life. God wanted me to put some action behind my faith, and my test was about to begin.

It is amazing what God does to get our attention, at times. I had become a very busy person; teaching full-time, training, being a father, and working in the family business meant I did not have much spare time. Life for me was fast-paced, but now, lying in this hospital bed, I had nowhere to go and all the time in the world to think. In the moment of solitude, while waiting patiently for the doctors and nurses to begin a number of tests on me, I found my mind wandering back to my childhood to a time and place where God was not welcome in our home.

As a young boy, I considered my father to be my hero, and I wanted to follow in his every footstep. But my father was an alcoholic, a chain smoker, had a foul tongue, and was a fighter. That was, until he met someone who would change his life radically, and that person was Jesus.

My father's example would serve as a visual example for me that anything was possible and that *yes, you can* do anything you want in life.

My father was born and raised in town called Runcorn, Cheshire, England. It was an industrial town that overlooked the banks of the River Mersey, which served as a cargo port. At a very young age, my father became very sick with kidney disease, and then to follow that, he got pneumonia, which was then followed by rheumatic fever. This series of events left my father paralyzed from the waist down for over a year. During those days in the early fifties, my father was placed in an isolation unit, and visitors had to wear gowns and masks just to visit with him. My grandparents had to travel an hour and a half by bus each way just to visit their son, but they were willing to do what it took to see my father through his time of suffering. Even though his parents didn't believe in God, my father had lots of time to think about his surroundings, such as the stars in the heavens that he could see from his hospital bed. His mother, during one of her visits, told my father that a little gospel hall church that was located at the end their street was praying for him, praying for his recovery. All these things told my father that there had to be a God. So at that young age, my father had this deep-down feeling that there was something greater than all this.

As time went on, my father learned to walk again. However, the effects of the rheumatic fever would leave my father with a heart mummer that would limit his chances of living very long. The outlook was not favorable. My father was told to get involved in sports activities such as running and swimming to help build up his heart, and that he did. He was never a shining star, but did enjoy the activities as he grew up to become a teen. Those teen years would cause his parents a lot of heartache and grief.

Being raised as a young boy during the fifties and sixties in Runcorn, my father would be best described as a hoodlum. He was always getting into trouble. His rebellious attitude would shine through on numerous occasions, including the time when he went to the very church his mother told him was praying for him when he was very sick, not to worship God, but just to throw a stone through the front window. There was no particular reason why he did this, other than it would be fun to do. As the stone shattered the window, an elderly gentleman of the church came running out looking for the culprit and after catching up with this hoodlum, he reprimanded him. This old man's final words were chilling and would leave an impression on my father that he would never forget. The elderly man said, "You know, you can be sure you are going to heaven one day, and all you need is Jesus in your life."

My father immediately said to himself, "Core Blamey, I thought the guy had gone barmy." (Old English words meaning that this old guy has gone off the deep end.) My father then ran away.

Years went on, and at the age of thirteen, my father was working delivering papers both morning and night. In those days, a train would drop off the newspapers, and the first boys to the train to scoop up the papers would have the better chance at getting more papers and selling them around the town. Fights would often break out among the boys over who got there first, but my father would often win. He was no pushover, and he was not afraid of hard work. My father was not shy about putting in long hours, even when everyone else his age was doing their own thing. He didn't mind the fact that he was different than most. Hard work seemed to run in his veins.

Scrapping and fighting with others was the norm in England. It was his lifestyle. It was something he did and did well. On one occasion during an altercation, my father was stabbed in the chest with a knife, followed by a severe beating, and then he was left to fend for himself. This was my father's lifestyle in England, and this was just the way things were at that point in time.

Academics did not suit my father, either. He had no time for that, and he would soon leave school at the age of fifteen to start learning a trade as a full-time machinist's apprentice. However, his life was without purpose and meaning. He knew there was more to life than living from paycheck to paycheck, spending all his money on booze and cigarettes, but he didn't know what it was that he was missing.

Being a teenager during the swinging sixties in Britain was an exciting time. The Beetles were just starting off in Liverpool, just miles away from Runcorn, and my father would often visit the pubs. Drinking, smoking, and cussing would become a way of life for him and his rebellious friends. On one particular evening, my father and his older sister walked into the Cavern Pub in Liverpool, the exact location the Beatles played, and it wouldn't be long afterward that his sister and he would have the entire bar in a fistfight. A young girl wanted to dance with my father, and my father's sister wanted no part of her dancing with her younger brother. So to stop this dance from happening, my father's sister punched this girl in the face, and moments later, launched the entire bar into an all-out brawl. This was the way of life for my father in Britain, and he didn't like it.

As an eighteen-year-old teenager, my father knew that his life was going nowhere, and he wanted out. Staying in Britain was not an option for him, and he wanted to move to the land of opportunity. His choice was simple: either move to Australia, or to Canada. Both promised a better life of opportunity.

As my father pondered his choice of countries, he did something strange. He took a coin and flipped it. If it landed heads-up, he would move to Canada, and tails-up meant a move to Australia. As fate, or rather God's hand, would have it, the coin landed heads-up, and so Canada it was. Against his parents' wishes, my father packed his bags and headed off to Canada. On November 9, 1965, my father landed in complete darkness at Pearson International Airport, in Toronto, Ontario, Canada, with a friend of his who also was leaving Britain to make a better life for himself. With less than one hundred dollars in his pocket and no place to stay, my father was ready to start his new life in Canada.

When my father was leaving the international airport in Toronto, the doors automatically swung open. This indeed was a strange sight for him, especially when he had never seen this before in England. My father pointed out to his friend that this country was much further ahead of Britain, and he liked it. While in Britain, he had heard of a city called Sarnia, Ontario, that had some job opportunities in the petrochemical industry, so with his friend in tow, they went to the Toronto train station to come to Sarnia, which was approximately 300 kilometers south of Toronto. The whole train terminal was lit with candles. My father was quite perplexed by what he saw after just being in the airport and said to his friend, "These guys don't even have lights. We are stepping back in time?" Little did my father know that night the whole northeastern seaboard had lost its power, due to a severe power outage that lasted several hours.

While in Sarnia that winter, my father was working repairing lake freighters that were laid up for the winter at the Sarnia docks. It would be a short time later when he would meet the girl of his dreams at a local A&W restaurant. My father saw this Chevy pull up and flash its lights to signal for service. In those days, the waitress would skate out to the cars on rollerskates and come to the window of your car and take your order. This Chevy car had two good-looking girls in it, and he took a liking to what he saw, so he boldly decided to get out of the car and go over and ask for a date. The answer was, "*Yes, you can*, take me on a date." Months later, they were married, and their first child would be born. On December 5, they had a baby boy named after him, Peter Wes Harding.

The happiness of a new child and their love for one another would soon be turned into bitterness and anger. As a young child, I remember watching my father drink and smoke like there was no tomorrow. My father loved his drink, and he always had a stash of alcohol in our basement. Because of his affinity for alcohol, we had little to no money as a family. My father loved his family, but he loved his drink more. The vices my father partook in were not good for his health or his marriage. My mother had threatened to leave my father on many occasions. On one occasion, she threw all of his clothes onto the lawn and left town. He had been out drinking all night, and my mother finally had enough. It was time for her to leave, and this fairy tale marriage was now on a collision course with disaster.

That was, until one day while listening to a radio broadcast in his car, he heard a local church was advertising a mid-week Bible study and was inviting people to attend. So my father decided to attend this mid-week Bible study and found out that they were just starting what they called "a new converts class." He was welcomed with open arms into this class. My father says the gospel was explained in such simplicity that night that he understood, for the first time in his life, that anyone could know for sure that they were going to heaven.

At that moment, my father was immediately drawn back to England and the words of the old gentleman that my father thought was "barmy" had finally come back to him. When looking back, my father knew God had a plan for his life, as He does for us all. My father knew that the Bible clearly stated that the Lord is not willing that any should perish, but that all should come unto Him, and we should sup with Him and Him with us. Yet God gave us all free wills to choose between life and death, forever with Him, or forever without Him.

That night, my father came to the realization that he needed God to fill the void inside of him. It was at that moment that my father accepted Christ as his personal Savior, and I remember my father being visibly repentant for the things he had done. My father was a new person now, and life would be different in the Harding home from that point forward. His old way of life was gone now, and the new had taken over. He now trusted in God for all things.

As a child, I vividly remember the radical change in his life that happened afterwards. I remember my father going into the basement and dumping over a thousand dollars' worth of alcohol down the drain (and that was back in the seventies). His cigarettes were gone, and his words were no longer seasoned with profanity. This change had an impact upon me as a child, and to this day my father has not had one drink or cigarette, since his new life began with God.

I now had a new father. A father devoted to doing things for his family and for God. My father's work ethic was second to none. He wanted to do the best job that he could and never sacrificed quality for quantity. My father would often say that God has given us one life to live, and we need to do all things well for Him. God would continue to test my father's faith, and each time my father would remain true to God. There would be many storms of life that my father would have to go through, but in each case, God carried him through, and each time my father would praise Him through the storm.

Over the years, my parents physically built three homes, including designing and building the home in which they currently reside. This was completed while they were working full-time, maintaining a family business, and raising five kids. My father often joked that my love for running started when I was young. When we would see him coming up towards the house on a Saturday morning, with a hammer in hand, we knew it was trouble. It meant work, and so our sprinting started—we ran and hid. When my father would enter the family room to find us, he often would find half-eaten apples and cans of pop half-drunk and no kids. He knew we had running in our blood.

God continued to bless my father in the years that followed, and the doors opened up at an oil refinery for a full-time job for my father. My father was to spend thirty-four years of his life working at this company, and in the last several years, he was promoted to a manager's position, a position held by people with engineers' degrees, not a grade ten high-school-dropout degree. Through it all, my father would often say to me, "I am a sinner saved by grace, blessed be the name of the Lord."

As I lay in the hospital bed, this memory served as a visual reminder to me that although God was silent at this moment, He was still there. I knew He was. Like during a rainstorm, the sun is still shining. Even though we cannot see it through the clouds, it is still there.

I was awakened from my thoughts as the nurse came back in the room and hooked up the third bag of IV fluids. She informed me that I was going to be leaving soon to get some tests done. She warned me that I was going to be pricked, poked, and prodded like never before. I had now taken priority over the rest of the patients, and the next few hours would promise to be busy. The nurse stated that my first destination would be getting an ultrasound done on my stomach. I was a little perplexed by this test, and I immediately said to the nurse that, "I am not pregnant. So why do I need an ultrasound?" I heard the nurse laugh as she walked out of the room. It was quiet again.

As I lay on my bed again, my mind wandered back to my childhood memories, and my mother came to mind. She was our rock and anchor of the family. She was always there and, like my father, she did not initially have a saving knowledge of Jesus Christ. By my father's radical change just a few days before, she, too, would ask God to be her forever friend. My mother was born and raised in Sarnia, Ontario, and grew up in a Catholic home. As the oldest of three children in her home, she would come to have many responsibilities placed upon her. She was a dedicated, loyal, and trustworthy girl who would also demonstrate an incredible work ethic.

My mother had an incredible influence upon us growing up. She not only loved the Lord God with all her heart, but she also placed a high priority on family. With her warm understanding and infinite patience, she always found time for us. Her heart was always filled with forgiveness when we, or others, had done something wrong, and she always had a word of encouragement for each one of us. Our home was brightened everyday by her smile and laughter. She was definitely a portrait of a godly woman, as found in Proverbs 31.

My mother was never idle. As long as I can remember, her hands were always busy, but she always found time for us. Having five children kept her busy. With four boys and one girl, she was found regularly praying on her knees for each one of us. There would never be a dull moment in the Harding home, and to keep herself busy during the quiet moments of the day, she bred dogs, English Springer and Cocker Spaniels. I can remember times when we would have dozens of puppies crawling all over us, and if that wasn't enough, she even started to operate her own janitorial business from our home, that would grow by leaps and bounds in the months to come. She was a strong, dignified multi-talented, caring woman who was after God's own heart. She, too, went through many storms of life, including breast cancer and the loss of her business by a devastating fire, but through it all, she trusted the Lord through the storm.

I was once again awakened from my moments of reflection by the nurse entering my room. Before I said anything to the nurse, I thanked the Lord for giving me such loving and caring parents, who would pave the way for me to dream big and to trust in the Lord in all things.

"Wow," said the nurse, laughing as she approached my bedside. "You are thirsty. We are now on the fourth bag of IV fluids, and you have only been here three hours. We are going to have to put in another order of IV fluids, just for you. Do you have to go to the bathroom, yet?"

"No, not at all" I said. I was glad I didn't have to, either, considering I was still attached to a multitude of wires and monitors. It sure would be an awkward sight, walking into the bathroom looking the way I did.

"But I am getting hungry," I gently hinted at her.

"There will be no eating for you, for a while. It's test time, now."

As I was wheeled down the hall into the ultrasound room, I was immediately thankful that I was still breathing. The hospital halls were filled with doctors and nurses running around, and some patients looked far worse than me.

"Okay, God," I said, "I don't know what is going to come from these series of tests, but I need you now more than ever." And again, God was quiet.

I knew God could do the impossible and raise me up. My strength was almost gone, but I knew He heard my heart cry. As my bed was wheeled into a dark, cool room filled with several ultrasound machines, I was now ready for the bad news.

I immediately asked what the purpose of the ultrasound was, to which the nurse replied that they needed to check my vital organs. As I watched her put the cold lotion on my stomach, a sense of awe came over me, and I saw my vital organs. What amazing technology! Beautiful pictures appeared before my eyes. I jokingly asked if I was missing any parts, and the nurse was in no mood to enjoy some humor.

She simply said, "Everything looks good here." Those words were music to my ears.

As the nurse rolled me out for my next appointment, she attached a new bag of IV fluids, before rolling me into the CAT (computer axial tomography) scan room. I once again felt important as the nurse outlined my agenda of the day for me. It was going to be a busy few hours of continuous testing. Something I was not looking forward to. She left me in the hall again, with complete strangers all around me, as I waited for the room to be ready for me. Once again, I questioned God, inquiring why He tests us and allows certain things to take place in a person's life.

As a Bible teacher in a private elementary school, I knew that God wanted us to be completely dependent on Him. I had often told my students the stories from the Old Testament where people were tested and tried. Stories like Abraham and Joseph, Moses, and King David, and many others who were tested for their faith. We find in scripture that testing is a catalyst that brings us to change. Often when we are riding the fence of faith, God can use tests to push us to the other side. We become who God wants us to become, only through trials and tests. He wants us to be completely dependent on Him, rather than going our own way. Through testing, our relationship can change from being distant to one of intimacy. And that is what I wanted.

I also knew that testing makes us stronger. Like steel, it must be put through a series of events to make it stronger. The hardness of steel is created by the degree at which it is heated and cooled. When it has been heated to an extreme temperature, it must then be immediately plunged into freezing cold water. When this takes place, the steel becomes stronger. Steel that has been slowly heated and slowly cooled is much softer.

As the apostle Paul says in James 1:2-4, "Consider it pure joy, my brothers, whenever you face trials of many kinds, because you know that the testing of your faith develops perseverance. Perseverance must finish its work so that you may be mature and complete, not lacking anything," (NIV). Paul had this figured out. Five times, he was lashed forty times, minus one, by the Jews. Three times, he was beaten with rods, and once he was stoned. Three times, he was shipwrecked, and was in danger many times by bandits, Gentiles and by his own countrymen. Paul definitely had a strong faith (2 Cor. 11:24-26).

I soon realized that my trials were nothing like Paul's, and yet he fought the good fight and finished the race. I knew that God already knew the outcome, and He already knew the person I was to become. So as the nurse walked by and attached IV bag number six to me, I came to the realization that God was bringing me to become the person He created me to be. A real peace came over me as the nurse pulled me into the room and injected a contrast dye into the vein in my arm. A warm feeling came over me, which was immediately followed by a metallic taste in my mouth. This was no steak dinner taste, but a taste that left a foul odor in my mouth. I thought I was really going to die after that injection, but the nurse reassured me that this dye would highlight areas in my chest, which would help create clearer images. For that, I was very grateful.

As the machine scanned my chest area, I felt a sense of peace come over me. I knew once again that, although I was not hearing God's small, still voice, I had seen that God has proven Himself though my parents' example, and that was enough evidence for me. As the nurse wheeled me down the hall to my room, I had this sense of urgency that I needed to go the bathroom. I was now on my seventh bag of IV fluids, and it had only been six hours. I came to the realization that I had gone through six liters of IV fluids. No wonder I needed to go. As I was wheeled back into my room, I mustered up my boldness to ask if I could go to the bathroom. Although a little awkward, it needed to be asked. At that moment, a call came through on the nurse's walkie-talkie that sounded urgent, which took priority over my question. The nurse quickly turned my bed around and started wheeling me back down the hall at a running speed. This confused me, so I asked the nurse where we were going.

"Back to the CT room," the nurse stated, "the doctors have found something, and they need to do another scan immediately!"

Oh, no, I thought. *Not another scan. Not another injection of that warm, metallic-tasting dye. This is turning out to be my horrible, no good, very bad day.* There was no waiting in the hall for the room this time. I was rushed right in. With a look of panic on the nurses' faces as they were running around setting up the CT machine for another scan, I immediately asked, "What's wrong?" As the nurse injected the dye into my arm again, I suddenly felt a warm panicking sensation come over me.

The nurse said, "We have found something, and it's serious."

As the CT scan machine began to hum, I began to sing.

MILE 80

A REFLECTION
THROUGH THE STORM

///

"It's not whether you get knocked down; it's whether you get up."

-*Vince Lombardi*

"I really do have to go to the bathroom," I said to the nurse as the CT scan machine started to hum for the second time. There was no shyness in asking now.

"We know," said the nurse. "We can tell by looking at the computer monitor."

Oh that's great, I thought. *There are no secrets now.* My mind wasn't so much on the bad news as it was on just finding a bathroom. As the scan was winding down, it was everything I could do just to grin and bear it. As the nurse rolled my bed out from the CT scan room, the rolling motion made it seem that much worse. I was never so glad to see my room. As I was moved into position in my room, the nurse gave me a bedpan and closed the curtain. "No privacy in the hospital room," I muttered. I now knew how women feel when they are about to give birth to a baby. No privacy anymore, I just wanted to be sure that the bedpan was going to hold it all.

The nurse graciously asked if I was finished, as my next appointment was awaiting me. It was a trip to the magnetic resonance imaging (MRI) room. The doctors had ordered an MRI scan on my right leg. Once again, I was in motion down the hall. I was getting quite comfortable being pushed everywhere and having a nurse wait on me hand and foot. I was thinking on route that I should suggest this to my wife, and then again, I thought I didn't want to be permanently injured and spend any more time in the hospital than I had to.

As the nurse rolled me into the MRI room, I found the machine quite intimidating. Like David meeting Goliath, I was ready for the challenge to take on this machine. After all, it felt as though I had been to every machine this hospital had to offer. The nurse had me roll from my bed onto another bed, which was going to be drawn inside a large, cylinder-shaped magnet. It looked like I was going to be inserted into the mouth of the beast. With a look of horror on my face, the nurse assured me that everything would be all right, and that this machine would be used to create pictures of tissues, organs, and other structures within the body. I was intrigued.

As the test was nearing completion, I once again was reflecting upon the events of the day. I had now been in the hospital nearly seven hours, and still I had no information as to what was wrong with me. I had hundreds of questions, but unfortunately, no answers. As I moved out of the MRI machine, my nurse assistant told me I had a cardiologist waiting to see me. The sound of her voice seemed to indicate that I was nearing the end of my travelling experience around the hospital. I was ready to eat, anyway, and I was looking forward to eating an all-you-could-eat, buffet-style dinner when I was finished with my next doctor.

As I was rolled once again down the hall, I was pleasantly surprised that the cardiologist was waiting for me. Usually whenever I have wanted to see a doctor, I would end up waiting patiently in a waiting room for hours on end for the doctor to become available. But this was not the case today.

"You are very fortunate to walk right in," announced the cardiologist. "There is currently a six-week waiting period for people to see me." I wasn't sure being here was good news or bad news, but I knew, regardless, God was watching over me.

"I need to check your heart right away," the cardiologist said in a hurried voice.

"Is everything okay?" I inquired. Everything was quiet as he was listening to my heart.

"We need to get you back to the ultrasound room. We have found something, but we won't know for sure until we double check." As he looked at the nurse, she started wheeling my bed out to the door. *Nothing like bedside manners,* I thought. No answers, just rushing around, it seemed. The journey back to the ultrasound room began.

As the nurse rolled my bed into the room with the ultrasound machines, I sensed we were getting closer to finding out what was wrong with me. "This is your last stop of the day," announced the nurse, as she turned and walked away. The time was now five o'clock in the afternoon, and I sensed the nurse using the ultrasound machine was in no mood for questions. By the look on her face, she was ready to go home, and so was I.

After five minutes of cold lotion and rubbing of the wand on my chest, the nurse had taken lots of pictures and video footage of my heart. The testing was now over. I quickly asked the nurse if I could get something to eat, since it had almost been twelve hours since I had last taken anything besides IV fluids into my body, and I was starving. I was reminded of my days as an overeating couch potato, and I was ready to chow down on some good hospital food.

Within moments, the nurse had returned with a sandwich in hand. "Is this all I get?" I asked politely of then nurse. I didn't want to sound like an ungrateful person, but I was famished. She assured me that I may have a cracker or two more, if I wanted it. "If I wanted it?" I whispered to myself. I needed it. The nurse then informed me of some more good news that I was not expecting. Although the testing was done for the day, the nurses still had to take blood from me every three hours.

Just when I thought things couldn't get worse, I was now informed that my sleep tonight would be interrupted by frequent periods of pricks and needles. The nurse then smiled at me, as if I was some sort of superstar when she said, "Do you realize you have gone through eight bags of IV fluids in eight hours? That is eight liters of fluid! You were really dehydrated. That is the most I have seen anyone take."

With a look of pride in my face I asked, "And what do I win for that?" After all, everything I do is a competition, and I am always looking for a prize.

"Well," she said, "your prize is another beautiful, silver bedpan, and I will leave it right here beside your bed."

I always love it when a plan comes together, except this was not the prize I wanted to win.

As the nurse was leaving the room, she turned and said as an afterthought, "Oh, yeah, the doctor has gone home for the night, and he will tell you tomorrow what you have." At that, she turned and shut the door.

What I have? I thought. It sounded to me like I had some sort of disease, or even worse. Could it be that this thing I had could deter me from my ultimate dream? Could it be that my dream was now over? A sudden feeling of panic overcame me as I lay in my bed listening to the voices of despair in my head. Could it really be that God was going to take this dream away from me? I was haunted by my thoughts.

As the sun was beginning to set, a ray of sunlight shone on my face. It was warm. It was bright. It was as if God Himself was there assuring me that I could trust Him. I knew that all things were possible with God, and that He could heal me of anything that I had. God had proven Himself over and over in my life, and why should I doubt His power now? I had seen God's hand upon my life many times, and each time, He would show me that He was in control, and He knew what was best for my life. As my mind started to wander back to those times, I found myself closing my eyes to envision God, my Father, right beside me in those times of despair and suffering.

The first test of my faith came when I was seventeen years old, when I was about to enter university. I chose to study commerce, and I was excited about the opportunities that would come because of that. That meant I would have to leave the security and comfort of my own home and start a new life for myself. I was informed by the university that my new home would be a co-ed residence, and from what I had heard, it had developed quite the name for itself over the years. It was known for its wild, all-night parities, drinking binges, and its girls. I had already seen the 1978 movie, *Animal House* starring John Belushi, and I envisioned lots of sleepless nights with roommates that are there for one reason only: to have a good time.

This really concerned me, because tuition to this university was very expensive, and I had to scrub a lot of toilets to pay for this education. I did not want to throw it all away on wild parties and wild friends. I knew I would need a solid roommate with the same morals and standards that I had. I needed a roommate who was hard working and ready to take on the world. What I didn't need was a roommate who would throw his year away, and his money, for a year-long party. Since this university had well over 20,000 people in it, I had no say in who my roommate would be. But I did know one person I could ask, and that was God.

So that summer before university began, I started to pray to God and ask Him to bring along the right roommate for me. I knew that if I didn't get the correct roommate, I could be swept away in the wild living and lose everything that I worked so hard to accomplish. Each and every night during the summer months, I would pray to God, earnestly asking Him for a roommate that would inspire and encourage me during the year.

The week before school started, my heart began to beat with incredible anticipation. What if God did not pull through for me? What if I got a roommate who wanted nothing to do with God, other than use His name in a creative way? Questions flooded my mind, and it was everything I could do to not think about it. It was all-consuming for me.

It was now Labor Day, fall was in the air, and my parents drove me over 200 kilometers to drop me off at my new home, the home of rock and roll. As we pulled into the residence, I saw thousands of students unpacking their life's possession from cars and guys holding up signs all around the dorm for parents to read that said, "If your daughter is a virgin today, she won't be tomorrow." *What kind of place was this?* I thought. My eyes were as wide as saucers. As I grabbed my suitcases with my parents in tow, I felt like a kindergarten student getting ready for his big day at school. My heart was beating like never before, as the smell of beer permeated the air. Beer cases were being piled to the ceiling, and the carpets were already soaked with alcohol. No wonder they called this co-ed residence the "animal house."

And there it was: my new room for the next year of my life. Like a car skidding out of control on a snowy road, I knew this was my moment. With all my might, I turned the door knob to my new destination, a destination that could end up in disaster. All was silent, all was empty. My new roommate had not arrived. I threw my things on my bed and kissed my parents goodbye. I knew it was hard on them, as well. I could tell by the look in their eyes. Their baby was leaving home, and they were dropping me off in a place of drugs, sex, and alcohol. I am sure they were just as anxious as I was and had to trust in the Lord that He knew best.

I no longer had my parents' faith to rely on. I would have to take ownership of that now and put my faith into action. I would have to trust God. As my parents shut the door of my room, I sat there quietly praying to God. Every movement outside the door would grab my attention, as if to say, this is it, you are about to find out your final destination. And then it happened, the door was about to be opened.

As I sat at the edge of my bed in anticipation of this moment I had been praying for, my new roommate entered the room. He was over six feet tall and had the build of a football player. I could tell by the look on his face that I was in trouble already. His stern look of disgust pierced my inner soul. As he threw his belongings on his bed he turned to me, looked me straight in my eyes and said something chilling to me, something I have never forgot to this day.

"Are you a Christian?" His words were seasoned with a tense muffle.

I found the question strange, especially when he didn't even give me a cordial greeting or introduce himself. I wasn't sure how to respond to this question. Was it a multiple choice question, A-yes, B-no, C-maybe, D-all of the above, E-what do you want me to say? As I looked at him, it was now my time to stand up for who I was and what I believed in. I had been rehearsing my answer now for ten years and have been praying for this moment for months. The moment of truth was about to be revealed.

"Yes, I am," I said with conviction and determination. Was a fight going to break out next? Was he going to turn around and walk out? Was he going to laugh at my answer? What came next was not what I was expecting at all.

He held out his hand and said, "Hi, my name is Jeff, and I have been praying for the last two months for a Christian roommate. In fact, so was my entire church of 5,000 members."

Wow, I thought, *who would have ever guessed that God was working behind the scenes in this way?* Little did I know, until this moment, that God had already planned everything perfectly. Should I have been surprised by the power of God? It was like I had won the lottery. My heart leaped for joy as I introduced myself.

Over the next several months, although the "animal house" was in a state of flux, Jeff and I would stand together and do the impossible. While the other students were having a good time, yet struggling in their

More potato chips, please! From triple chin to Ironman.

Before (age 40) and after (age 44).

Dream #1: Finishing my first marathon at the age of 41.

Silver medal winner at the "Around the Bay" 30K race in Hamilton, Ontario.

Love at first sight! My parents on their wedding night, June 17, 1967.

After 25 years, the thriving Harding family business was totally destroyed by a vicious fire.

The family business lay in ruins.

Dream #2: Graduating from the University of Windsor at the age of 42, celebrating with my parents, Betty and Peter Harding.

Dream #3: Running the Boston Marathon.

Dream #4: Running the Boston Marathon with my hero and inspiration, Dick Hoyt.

Uta Pippig, Olympian and 3-time winner of the Boston Marathon and coach of Team Hoyt.

The Harding girls and Rick Hoyt before the Boston Marathon!

Team Hoyt, with Dick and Rick Hoyt, on the starting line of the 116th Boston Marathon.

The dream is finally realized. Resting on the finish line of the Boston Marathon.

After the Boston Marathon race, a "Fenway Ballpark" hot dog. The envy of Rebekah, Ciera, and Anissa.

The Harding family in Lake Placid, New York.

Anissa cheerleading in Lake Placid.

Anything is possible! Jessica and "Wes You Can" at The Lake Placid, Ironman Triathlon.

Dream #5: From coach potato to Ironman.

My biggest cheerleader, my wife and best friend, Sue, overlooking Lake Placid, New York.

Dream #6: Running as an angel with myTEAM TRIUMPH, West Michigan Chapter.

Dream #7: Working with my friend and author, Todd Civin, on this book.

Mayor Mike Bradley of the City of Sarnia, Ontario, presenting the Mayor's Honor Award 2012 for making a difference in the community.

classes, we were having a great time, yet doing exceptionally well in ours. That year changed me. It proved to me that God could do anything.

As I closed my eyes, I remembered a time of blessing that occurred after this trial during university, and this blessing would carry on in the years that followed. I knew God delighted in blessing His children, and I was about to be blessed, indeed. God was about to introduce the woman of my dreams to me. This girl was to become my greatest encourager, friend, confidant, wife, and mother to our children.

During the end of my second year at university, some of my college friends wanted me to go on a spiritual college retreat with them that would be held on the first weekend of June. This thought really didn't suit me well, considering that work came first. I really did not have any time to get away, and the thought of spending a weekend with a bunch of guys didn't really suit me that well.

After days of pestering, my friends finally enticed me to go when they said, "There are some really good-looking girls that will be there!"

That little bit of incentive was all I needed to go, as I immediately said to them, "Sign me up. When do we leave?"

As I jumped into my friend's car that Friday afternoon and headed off to a campground named Silver Lake, I was preparing for the worst. Good-looking girls were a matter of perspective, and although I was looking for no one in particular, I knew God would bring me the perfect one, in His timing.

As we arrived, we unpacked our things in our cabin and went to the mess hall to meet everyone else. There were approximately fifty college students there in attendance, and as we sat down to hear our first speaker for the weekend, it happened. It really was love at first sight. As my head scanned the college students in attendance, I had to do a double take. There she was, this good-looking girl whom I had never seen before. My heart was telling me, this is the one, this is the one! I was quite taken aback by her dark hair and brown eyes. Her appearance was very attractive, as the light from the fireside radiated around her.

She is mine, I thought to myself. During the course of the presentation from our first speaker, I thought out my plan of attack on how I would introduce myself. I was counting down the minutes when the speaker would conclude, and then I could make my move.

As fate would have it (or was it the hand of God?), I made a beeline to this girl. With my sweet British accent (I don't have a British accent, but accents sometimes work for the best, as in this case), I introduced myself to this girl. Her name was Suzie, and to my surprise she lived in a small farming community about 60 kilometers from my home. *How convenient this is,* I thought. As the small talk began, I found myself in heaven, talking to an angel and the girl of my dreams, all at the same time. *This is going to be a great weekend,* I thought to myself. That was, until my friend said something that changed everything.

As we were leaving to our cabins that night, my friend whom I came with said to me, "I saw you talking to my girlfriend. So what do you think of her?" I was horrified. I couldn't believe my luck. She already had a boyfriend, and it was my friend who invited me to this retreat. *That's it,* I thought. *It's game on, friend or no friend, it is time to make my move.* Mario Andretti, the NASCAR race driver, was right when he said, "Desire is the key to motivation, but its determination and commitment to an unrelenting pursuit of your goal— a commitment to excellence— that will enable you to attain the success you seek." And I was determined to seek out the girl of my dreams. It was desire, all right. That was my motivation, and my friend had never seen my unrelenting pursuit.

As we headed back to the mess hall the next morning for breakfast, the pursuit was on. The stakes were high, so I had to make the first good impression. After breakfast, I did something I normally did not do. As the guys headed off together, I grabbed a towel and started drying the dishes with the girls. This move got Suzie's attention. How many guys are manly enough to do the dishes? I was, and this got me talking to Suzie again.

That afternoon, we had free time as a group. So we all decided to go canoeing. I could tell by the look in Suzie's eyes, she had a thing for me. So I quickly informed everyone that I was going to be partners with Suzie. Unfortunately, that was the wrong answer, as I was informed that her boyfriend had already asked her.

As she jumped into the canoe with her boyfriend, I was all eyes on them. Nothing was going to escape my view, as I jumped into another canoe and followed closed behind. *This is not where I want to be,* I thought to myself. I needed to be quicker and make the most of every situation, especially when we only had another twenty-four hours left at the retreat.

After the canoe ride, we all went back to the mess hall for supper. Following supper, I was more determined than ever to win her heart. I always knew, as old Englishman Thomas Fuller once said, "An invincible determination can accomplish almost anything, and in this lies the great distinction between great men and little men." And I had a little English blood within me, so I was ready for my next move.

After the speaker had ended that evening, we decided to do something a little strange. It was the first weekend in June, and the cool spring breezes were still blowing. There was talk about going to a little sauna hut out near a small pond, and so it was decided that we would grab our bathing suits and head out to the sauna. *Perfect,* I thought. Not only would I get to see the girl of my dreams in her bathing suit, but it was also my perfect time to make my grandest move of all on her. My timing had to be perfect, otherwise it would not work.

We all rendezvoused at the sauna, and it was now nearing midnight. The sauna hut was just starting to warm up. I could already tell I was warming up, too; I was warming up to my plan of attack. As we sat there as a group, laughing and having a good time, Suzie decided to go outside and cool down. As she stepped off the ledge and headed for the door, I knew that this was my time to make my move. It was now or never. With my heart beating faster than ever, I followed her out through the door. She stopped just at the edge of a small dirty pond filled with weeds. I went up beside her and did something a little uncharacteristic of me. I needed to get her attention and make her notice me. The stakes were high, and it was winner take all now, so I picked up Suzie in my arms and threw her into the middle of the pond.

With a splash, Suzie came running out of the pond and jumped right into my arms (well not exactly). She hit my arm and said to me, "What did you do that for?"

"I wanted to cool you down," I said, and as Paul Harvey, that great American storyteller would say, "And now you know the rest of the story." For it would only be hours later that Suzie and I would be exchanging phone numbers and addresses, and come to find out, she wasn't dating my friend as I had been led to believe! Two years later, we would be married on June 16, 1990. I married my best friend, my gift from God. It was a marriage made in heaven and lived out on earth. And so our family began when, two years later, our first daughter was born. That would once again test our faith in God.

This test would leave us wondering if all things were possible with God. In 1992, when we were both twenty-four years old, our first daughter, Rebekah, was born. Her name meant "to bind," and by her kindness and generosity, she would bind our family together. This was our first gift from God, and the moment of celebration immediately turned to a moment of concern for us, as we learned that our newborn daughter's legs did not bend like a normal individual. Instead, Rebekah's legs bent the opposite way.

The doctors shared with us the rather depressing prognosis that she would probably never walk like everyone else. A moment of fear embraced us as we stood face-to-face with the reality that we could have a disabled daughter, who could spend the rest of her life in a wheelchair. A surgical pediatrician was summoned twenty-four hours later to assess our new pride and joy. In our despair, we cried out to God to heal our daughter, and we also shared this news with our own church and asked the members to pray. Prayer had always been a powerful tool in our lives, and we needed it now more than ever. When the nurse came to take Rebekah from our room to see the surgeon, we knew that she was in God's hands. This was His baby girl, and all things were possible with Him. God had a plan for her life.

As parents, we were confused when, within minutes, the nurse would return Rebekah to us. The nurse stated something that we never forgot as she said, "Someone has been praying for Rebekah."

As we began to comprehend her statement, she continued by saying that when the doctor examined Rebekah, he had asked the nurse if this was "some type of a joke." The doctor was not pleased with her humor as there was absolutely nothing wrong with Rebekah. Her legs bent just like everyone else's and, in that moment, we knew that the hand of the Lord was upon Rebekah. We had felt and seen His power. He was still in the business of performing miracles. Today, Rebekah is twenty years old, and nothing stops her!

It would be only ten months later we would be tested once again with the most challenging of life's tests. On March 16, 1993, a son, Peter Nathanael, was born to us. The dream of having the million dollar family had now come true for us. We now had the perfect family, a daughter and a son. The world was ours, and we gave praise to God. Unfortunately, the celebration of a new son ended a few short hours later, as we learned that God had a different plan. Although Nathanael was born on earth, God was going to raise him in heaven. Nathanael died due to breathing problems.

The news of our son's passing away was heartbreaking. Tears flowed like never before. Our hearts were crushed, as life would now be different. I knew I had to do one thing for my son; I built his casket. As the tears poured on the wood of that little box, I knew God had a greater plan, although it was difficult to conceive at that time what that plan was.

On the day of the burial, the cool March winds blew through the barren trees around the gravesite. With not a leaf on the tree, it reminded us that everything had a season. As King Solomon so eloquently said in

Ecclesiastes 3, "There is a time for everything; a time to be born and a time to die," but we didn't realize that the season for the life Nathanael had was going to be so short. As a witness to all who would pass by his tombstone, the words from Mark's gospel were inscribed on his tombstone in which Jesus says, "Suffer the little children to come unto me and forbid them not, for of such is the kingdom of Heaven," (Mark 10:14, KJV). The verse continues, "And Jesus took them up in his arms, put his hands upon them, and blessed them." We knew that Nathanael was in a much better place than what this world could ever offer. It was difficult to see God's vantage point as to why He allowed Nathanael to die.

There were showers that day as we placed that little coffin in the ground; they were showers of tears and sorrow. Job, the suffering servant said it best when he said, "The Lord gave, and the Lord hath taken away; blessed be the name of the Lord," (Job 1:21b, KJV). And so we trusted and sang the blessings of the Lord.

It would only be fourteen months later when we would truly understand the plan of God, and the blessing of the Lord would be experienced in a mighty way. On May 2, 1994, God gave us a beautiful baby girl, whom we would name Jessica, which means "God's gracious gift." Jessica was our gift from the Lord, and we praised God each and every day for our special gift, Jessica. We had no intent on ever having another child, but in God's divine power, He had a different plan for us, and we now look back and say to ourselves that we really like God's plan. It was the best.

Our third blessing would come another two years later, and on June 20, 1996, a new baby girl would be born to us. Her name would be Anissa, which means, "God has favored us." God has indeed favored us with three beautiful girls, and we thought our family was now complete. Little did we know that God had another surprise in store for us.

On January 13, 1999, God saw fit to give us another baby girl. Her name was to be Ciera which means "angel." She was our special angel given to us to make our home complete. Being the youngest with three older sisters is not an easy task, but one she does quite well, considering she is an angel. With God's "binding," His "gift," His "favor," and His "angel," we now had the four-million-dollar family.

There seems to be a widespread mindset that children are a bother, an expense, or liability, an obstacle that hinders their parents' success and enjoyment in life, but we saw it differently. We saw it as the blessing of the Lord upon us. As the Psalmist so correctly put it in Psalms 127:3-5, we were blessed, as the writer said, "Behold, children are a gift of the Lord, the fruit of the womb is a reward. Like arrows in the hand of a warrior, so are the children of one's youth. How blessed the man whose quiver is full of them; they will not be ashamed when they speak with their enemies in the gate," (NAS). In essence, the author of this verse is stating metaphorically that, whatever life throws at you, a solid family brings strength, stability, preparedness. And the enemy is the storms of life which you will be able withstand as a family. The phrase "quiver full" is a relative term, but in hunting terms, especially bow hunting, the arrows are carried in a tubular item called a quiver, and in the days gone by, the hunters quiver could hold five arrows: five arrows filled the quiver. The arrows represent our children that we shoot off into the world. For our family, we had a hunter's quiver of children: Rebekah, Nathanael, Jessica, Anissa, and Ciera, who would go off into the world to a time and place that we could not go to.

As I reflected upon the trials and blessings of the Lord in the solitude of my hospital room, I came to the realization that God hasn't left us, and whatever the outcome was to be in the morning, I would trust that He would know what was best me for. Before closing my eyes to go to sleep, I said, "Thank you, Lord, for what You have done in my life and what You are about to do in the days ahead." It didn't matter what the outcome was going to be in the morning, I just knew it was God's plan.

"Okay, God, I have one life to live, and into Your hands I place my life. You are the potter, and I am the clay. Mold and shape me into the person You want me to be, but use a little water on me when You shape me."

MILE 90

NEVER SAY NEVER

"Teach us to use wisely all the time we have. When morning comes, let your love satisfy all our needs. Then we can celebrate and be glad for what time we have left."

-Psalms 90:12,14

As the nurse pricked my arm to draw some more blood, I saw that the doctor and cardiologist whom I had seen the previous day were standing over me. In my humor, I asked which doctor brought the coffee. In their smiles, they began sharing the news that I so longed to hear.

The emergency doctor began by saying that, in my collapse, I had not suffered a heart attack at all, but rather I had suffered a severe form of dehydration. It was so severe that my kidneys had begun to shut down, and the other organs were starting to do the same. Since there was not enough water in my body, the kidneys, knowing they weren't needed, would be the first to malfunction. When I was rushed in the day before, their main concern was to immediately hydrate me with as much IV fluids as my body was willing to take, in order to get the kidneys back up and running. Their next step was to ensure that my internal organs had sustained no damage, hence, the ultrasound test. There was no evidence that any damage had been done to my organs as a result of dehydration. A moment of celebration came over me, but was soon stopped as the cardiologist began his diagnosis.

He began to share that the cardiac enzyme that was being sent from my heart indicated that I had suffered severe muscle damage. Cardiac enzymes are proteins from heart muscles that are released into the bloodstream when heart muscle is damaged. By measuring blood levels of cardiac enzymes, doctors can tell whether heart muscle damage has recently occurred. The good news was my heart muscle was okay, but my leg muscles were not. Because of the severe dehydration, the muscles did not have what they needed to do the job of running, hence the sharp pain that was shooting through my leg as I entered the park. An orthopedic surgeon would have to be called in to examine my leg to see whether or not I would need surgery to repair the damaged knee.

As the doctors paused to look at each other, I sensed the climax of my diagnosis was coming. I took a moment to compose myself, as well as reflect upon the doctor's statements. I knew I'd hurt my knee, but being laid up in a hospital bed and not walking for the past twenty-four hours, I did not realize just how badly it was damaged. This was cause for concern, but then I heard the cardiologist's crackling voice as he said, "We did find something wrong with your heart. You have heart valve disease."

"Heart valve disease," I said. "How is that possible?"

"Well, it is possible," he said, "you were probably born with it. As far as we can tell, you have had it your entire life. You are a very lucky man. Most people die from this without even realizing they have it. Since we know you have it, we can monitor it and treat it, if need be. You are very fortunate indeed that this happened to you. We believe you need surgery to correct this, but we are sending you to a university hospital to get a second opinion."

I never saw that coming. This was all new to me, as I asked what heart valve disease was.

The cardiologist patiently explained, "Heart valve disease occurs if one or more of your heart valves doesn't work the way they should. The heart is made up of four chambers and maintains one-way blood flow through the heart. The four heart valves make sure that blood always flows freely in a forward direction and that there is no backwards leakage. In your case, one of your valves is not working properly and causes leakage in a chamber. There are different severities of heart valve disease, mild, moderate, and severe. We believe, in your case, you have a moderate-to-severe case of heart valve disease, but we are sending you to another cardiologist for a second opinion."

Not being educated in the field of health, I was confused and perplexed by the cryptic statements made by the doctors I had just heard. What did this all mean? For me, it really boiled down to one question: would I ever be able to run again? As I turned to look at the doctors, they had already sensed my first question, and they replied that they didn't know the answer to this question, yet, until a second opinion could be given. As the doctors left me alone in my room, I closed my eyes and prayed for God to do His miracles again, like He had done so many times before in my life. As I lay there, a calm feeling came over me, reassuring me that God would work out all things for His glory.

I knew His power was tested and tried on several occasions like the time, when Sue and I were just married. God had blessed us with a small home in a little community called Forest, Ontario. We had no idea why God wanted us in Forest, as we were looking at getting an apartment in Sarnia, approximately 50 kilometers south of Forest. We were excited for our new home, but because both of us were working in Sarnia, and attending church there as well, that meant we both would have to drive half an hour to Sarnia and half an hour back. This meant an extra expense for us as a young couple starting in life, and it meant our time as well. But we believed that this was where God wanted us, and we were committed to it. It would be ten months later when we would finally know why God had called us to live in this small community.

It all started with a knock on our front door on a Saturday morning. As I opened the door, a man in his mid-fifties would introduce himself as the pastor of the local community Baptist church in town. He continued by saying that, even though he did not know who I was, nor I know him, God had revealed to their church that I would be their next part-time youth pastor. I was amazed. I did not even attend this church, nor did I even know most of the members of this church. The pastor then went on to say that their church had been looking for a part-time youth pastor for several months. They had interviewed several prospective candidates, but with each one God was telling them no. The search committee of this church felt it was now time to follow God's lead and ask me.

I was quite taken aback by this pastor's story and me being the youth pastor for their church. I had gone to university to be an elementary school teacher, not work with teenagers. I never wanted to do that. As we sat together in our kitchen, I asked the question, "How do you know it is me that is meant to take the roll of leading the youth, when you don't even know me?"

His answer stopped me in my tracks, when he replied, "Because God told us you were the one."

"Wow," I said. "That's incredible." I had never heard the audible voice of God before, but I knew that God worked in mysterious ways. So I told him I would pray about this, and the pastor went on his way.

As my wife and I sat in the kitchen, we both marveled at how God worked. Could it be that this is why God had allowed us to purchase this quaint little home in this community? I knew that I wanted to teach, so maybe this is where God was calling me. I had decided, after graduating from university, that I wanted to teach in the public school system, but unfortunately, for the past year, the doors were closed. We often questioned ourselves as to why God would allow me to get my degree and not let me be used in the public school system. *Maybe this is why,* I thought, *and maybe this is why God allowed us to purchase this home.* It was to be used as a gathering place for the teenagers in the youth group. Because there were no jobs in the teaching profession, I was working full-time at my parents' business, making good money, and this part-time youth pastor position would definitely allow me to teach young people.

After several days of waiting upon the Lord, it was revealed to us both, Sue and I, that I was to be the next youth pastor at this church. As I called the pastor up, I had an incredible sense of peace that this is where God was calling me at this point in time. The pastor was overjoyed in hearing the news, and after a short interview, I was brought before the church so the members could vote on my position.

The voting was to be held that Sunday, and with great anticipation, we met its members and were approved. The vote was unanimous. I was to be their new youth pastor.

I would spend the next six years at that small community Baptist church as youth pastor, and in those years, I learned so much about teaching. The youth were incredible; they taught me to become the person I am today. Those years, along with the guidance of this amazing pastor, served as the building blocks for my speaking and teaching ability. I made many mistakes during those years, but the pastor and the members of the church were so gracious to me. They continued to inspire me that, yes, I could do this and I could do it well.

I remember as a young pastor at this church, my speaking ability was not well-developed. I got really nervous and stuttered every time I got up in front of the church to give announcements or read scripture on Sunday mornings. In fact, I dreaded it. Speaking in front of large groups was not something I did well, and I did not enjoy it, but it was part of the job, and I had to do it.

On this one particular Sunday, the pastor had called me up at home and announced to me that I would be reading from the book Matthew.

The passage of scripture would be taken from Matthew chapter one. A feeling of panic fell over me as I put down the phone, and I realized that Matthew chapter one contained the genealogy of Jesus. That chapter contained Hebrew names I knew I could never pronounce. As I turned to that chapter, I knew I was done. I couldn't do it. There was no way I could say, with correct pronunciation, the names of these individuals leading up the birth of Christ. It was impossible; I told my wife that I never could read that passage.

As I sat at the edge of the bed in preparation for this horrific event of reading names, I knew I couldn't pronounce them, but my wife encouraged me that I could do it, and it wasn't that hard. As I slowly read through each verse, I then came to the very word which I knew meant disaster. I could never pronounce this name. The name was found in verse eight, the name was "Jehoshaphat." As best as I tried, I could not pronounce this name correctly. I was done for and I knew it, and there were sixteen more verses after that.

My wife saw the look of defeat on my face and quietly came by my side and looked at the word I was stuck on. In her reassuring words, she said that it was easy to remember. Just think of it as "Joe-hoe-so-fat."

So I was ready! As the pastor called me up that Sunday, the audience became hushed as the scripture was about to be read. I could hear a pin drop, and the creaking of the old wooden floors of that church reminded me with each step that this was my time, as I walked to the front of the church.

As I stepped up to the pulpit, I felt the stares of every eye on me. I was nervous, and my cheeks glowed with the heat that was radiating from my face. As I began to read, I kept rehearsing over and over in my mind that one word I knew was coming, "Joe-hoe-so-fat." And then it happened: it was now time to read verse eight. Like a boy getting ready to jump over a puddle, I paused, took a breath, and began to read the name. And then I panicked. I couldn't do it. I started stuttering this name that I had been practicing all morning. I was so embarrassed. In my moment of haste, I looked up at the audience before attempting the word again, and then I saw him. His name was "Joe" and he was a farmer in our community. He was an usher that morning and the word I was so greatly struggling with came to me as I said, "Joe-is-so-fat." The audience erupted into uncontrollable laughter and then turned their heads to look at Joe as he stood at the back of the room.

I couldn't believe I said that. Joe couldn't believe I said that. The damage was done. How could I ever recover reading from this disastrous moment? I was humiliated. I was done for. I never wanted to speak in public, ever again. I looked at farmer Joe as his face turned beet-red with embarrassment. Farmer Joe then did something I was not expecting, he smiled. At that moment of forgiveness, I knew I had a friend for life. After the laughter finished, I went on to finish off the names with complete clarity. I was able to do the impossible, although not perfectly. I had read the genealogy of Jesus.

This event reinforced in my mind that, "It's not whether you get knocked down; it's whether you get up." I was knocked down that morning, and I had a choice to make; I could walk away in defeat, or I could get back up and make a difference. I went to farmer Joe after the morning service to apologize to him and in his meek spirit, said to me, "There is no need to apologize. That was funny."

That moment would be etched in my mind forever. This experience would serve as a gentle reminder to me that, when the winds from the storms of life knocked you down, get back up.

A smile came over my face, and the nurse standing over my bedside realized that I was having a party inside of my head. She looked at me and smiled as she said, "Is everything alright?"

"Everything is fine," I said. "Everything is just fine!"

"You are an unusual patient," the nurse said. "Most patients would be upset about what they have just heard from the doctor."

"Not me," I replied. "I will be fine. God has it all worked out."

The nurse adjusted my bedside and left me there in my solitude. I knew she sensed she was disturbing something so beautiful—my thoughts. On her way out, she said, "You can trust Him. He does know best."

As I thought upon her statement, "You can trust Him," I was drawn to a moment in the past when I really did have to trust Him.

It was summer. The year was 1993, and I received a call that changed the course of my life. It was a Christian education pastor from my previous church. They had just started up a Christian school and were looking for a teacher for the seventh and eighth grade class. I was ecstatic when I heard that, once again, my name had come up in their search for a new teacher, especially when I did not even apply for the position. This was what I had been waiting a long time for: a job teaching full-time in a school setting. Without hesitation, I informed this pastor I would love to be considered for the job, to which he responded by setting up a time to interview me. After I hung up the phone, I shouted to my wife from the top of my lungs that I might have a job teaching at a school. Words could not contain my excitement. This was what I was called to be. This was what I was called to do.

The interview was to be held at Pizza Hut. I found this quite unique, but nevertheless, it didn't matter, and with my resume in hand, I went expecting to be hired. As I sat down at the table with this pastor, he began sharing the vision of the school and what I would be doing at the school. I could not believe what I was hearing. It had almost sounded like I had the job. Before the pastor could go any further, I asked him if I had the job. To my surprise, he said, "Of course you do. The job is yours."

Wow! I couldn't believe it. I asked the pastor how he got my name, and then I heard it again. "God told us," he said. Just when I thought things couldn't get any better. I was shell-shocked by his response. It had sounded exactly like the same discussion and answer the other pastor gave me from the small community church, when they were looking for a youth pastor. Once again, I have never heard God speak audibly to me before, but I knew God was calling me to this job. I accepted the job, and life was good.

As I walked through the front door, I announced to my wife that she was now looking at a new teacher. She was overjoyed that I was finally going to do what I was called to do: teach. Like any good wife, she asked me what I was getting paid to do this job. To which I responded, "I don't know, I didn't ask." But that didn't matter, did it? I had the perfect job. As I pondered her words, a dose of reality hit me. I needed to know how much I was getting paid. I had bills to pay, and I had to support my family.

I immediately got on the phone and called the Christian education pastor. When he answered the phone, I asked, as an afterthought, "How much am I getting paid?"

There was an eerie silence on the phone, when he said, "We can only pay you $24,000 per year." At that moment, I dropped the phone. I couldn't believe what I just heard: $24,000 per year! I had a mortgage payment to make, two car payments, a family, and utilities to pay that amounted to much more than $24,000. I would never be able to survive on that pay. I turned and looked at my wife as I picked up the phone, and with a look of defeat on my face, I said to the pastor, "I am sorry, but I cannot accept this position. You might want to find someone else."

My heart was crushed and broken. How could this be? I thought I had the perfect job, teaching. I knew when you found something you enjoyed doing, you would never have to work a day in your life, and teaching was what I enjoyed doing. I was devastated. That afternoon, in my despair, I found myself questioning God.

That evening, I had a party to attend. It was a BBQ that was being held by my banker. He was the manager at our local bank and oversaw all of my accounts. I was working full-time at my parents' business, making good money, and working part-time as a youth pastor. Life was good, and my banker knew that. The income from both positions gave us security in knowing there would be food on the table for tomorrow.

As we were welcomed at his home, I was impressed by his humility and wisdom. He was certainly a man of stature. As we sat around the fire pit after dinner, I ventured to tell him the story that had just transpired earlier in the day. I thought this story of being offered a full-time teaching position and only getting paid very little would arouse some humor and laughter for the night. His reaction was not what I was expecting. In fact he had my attention.

His next few words would become ingrained in my memory for the rest of my life. I knew he was a man of wisdom, but I was not anticipating his next sentence. Through the fire, my banker looked straight into my eyes and said in his stern voice, "Do you trust God?"

Whoa, I thought. *Where did this come from?* "Of course I do," I responded, returning fire for fire. "I am the youth pastor at the church." I expected that sentence to end all sentences.

Then he said it, those very words I knew were not possible. "Then do it. Take the job!"

"But, Dave," I responded, "you out of all people know that this is not possible! You know my accounts, and you know I cannot survive on this little pay."

I don't know what I was expecting him to say at this point, but he said it again, this time with more emphasizes, "Do you trust God?"

At that moment, I realized what my banker was saying. I didn't trust God. If I had trusted God, then I would have taken this position, especially when I knew within my heart this was the position for me. I looked at my banker as he said, "Then do it."

I went home that night and did something I had never done before. I fell on my knees and asked God to forgive me. I didn't trust Him, and after seeing His power over and over again, I knew He could do the impossible. God could provide all my needs, and although I could not see how that was possible, I knew He was a great God.

The very next day, I called the Christian education pastor up again and asked him if the job was still available. To my delight, it still was and I accepted. I knew I would have to leave the comforts of the family business and go to a place where God had called me. Not knowing how He was going to provide, made me realize that was called faith.

Faith is complete trust and confidence in someone or something, a firm belief in something for which there may be no tangible proof. Faith is the opposite of doubt, which I had. I realized I had doubted that God could provide for me if I accepted this job. As the writer of the book of Hebrews states in Hebrews 11:1, "Now faith is being sure of what we hope for and certain of what we do not see," (NIV). I had to completely put my trust in the Lord for Him to work out all things, including my finances. The writer of Hebrews continues by saying, "And without faith it is impossible to please God, because anyone who comes to Him must believe that He exists and that He rewards those who earnestly seek Him," (NIV). I was ready to trust God, and I wanted to experience the blessing of the Lord upon me and my family.

As I pushed myself up on the bed to look out the window, I came to the realization that event happened seventeen years early. I had been teaching at this same school that long, and what a faith walk it has been. God had not only provided for all my needs, but blessed me beyond my wildest imagination. Not once over those seventeen years have I found myself wanting. I have been blessed in ways I never thought possible. All things were possible for God, and this experience would be one more way for God to prove Himself.

At that moment, the doctor came into my room with the news I had been waiting so patiently for. It was music to my ears, when he said, "You can go home now. We have set up an appointment with a cardiologist in London for you, and from there, you will hear back from us by the end of the week. You also have an appointment with the orthopedic surgeon tomorrow, back at this hospital. In the meantime, you will need the use of these crutches to move around."

I was pleased to hear I finally could go home. Food, sleep, and the comforts of home now satisfied me. *It's kind of funny*, I thought. *You really don't appreciate the simple things in life, until you lose them.* It would be good to get home—after all, a man's castle is his home—and besides, my cheerleaders where all waiting to see me, just like at the finishing line.

As I adjusted the pillow on the couch, I came to the conclusion that I needed to live life like it was my last and make the most of every opportunity. My next breath could be my last. It is time to make a difference, and a difference we will make!

"Okay, God," I said. "If I can't run anymore, You will just have to push me in my wheelchair!"

And I heard a small, still voice say, "We will do it together. It's time to get back up!"

MILE 100

PUSHING THE LIMITS

> *"That which doesn't kill us makes us stronger."*
>
> *-Friedrich Nietzsche*

I admit it, I am a wimp when it comes to pain. On a scale of one to ten, my pain tolerance is zero. My wife would tell you that, with any discomfort beyond a pinch, I become a big baby. However, the injuries I have faced over the past few years have taught me that I need to learn how to face challenges, and those challenges often involve discomfort and pain.

During my forty-five years on this planet, I have found that life never gets easier. You just get stronger. No one likes the word "pain" or even the thought of experiencing it. Pain is a word that is associated with hurt, discomfort, and distress, or in some cases agony. Pain comes in many feelings. It could be steady and constant, like in a headache, or it could be that throbbing or pulsating pain. It could even have that stabbing or pinching sensation. Pain is an individual experience, and its tolerance varies from person to person. But most people don't associate pain as being a gift or being something good.

The purpose of pain is to motivate a person to withdraw from damaging situations; it protects that particular body part while it heals. Pain entices us to avoid similar situations in the future.

As I sat on my comfy couch waiting for my next appointment with the cardiologist from London to give me his diagnosis on my condition, I considered the pain I had experienced in the past twenty-four hours. How much more pain would I need to take before I could realize the dream of meeting the qualification times to run the Boston Marathon?

Over the course of the few races I had run up to this point, I had found that competitive runners often flirt with the red line between pure, unadulterated pain, while other runners strive for something less severe, something between no pain and a little discomfort. This is the great divide that separates the mediocre runners from the exceptional ones. After running my last half-marathon, I noticed that experienced runners were used to discomfort, almost to the point that pain was their training companion. Watching quality runners run those blazing speed sessions and killer hill workouts, or even those long three hour runs to come back exhausted, but with a smile on their faces, said to me that there is value in pushing yourself to the next level. There is joy in suffering. This venturing out to the threshold of pain is what I realized *Nietzsche was saying when he said, "What doesn't kill you makes you stronger." To win races, you needed to push yourself to the next level, and that might mean that you may experience some pain along the way. For me, I wanted to be stronger, I wanted to be faster, but I knew I had to start training smarter.*

I was no longer an overweight, overeating couch potato of 220 pounds, but now in my attempt to get faster I went to the opposite extreme of losing too much weight, and not only did my weight drop drastically, but my eating habits suffered severely as well. I had lost almost 80 pounds since I had begun running, and I was getting weaker and slower, instead of faster. I assumed that lighter meant faster, but that was not the case. I looked thin, frail, and rather sickly. I knew this: I heard the rumors in the parking lot from the parents of the students at school who said I looked like I had cancer or that I was dying from a strange disease. Whatever the case, I did not look well, and everyone had noticed. And after experiencing what I did in my last race, I had finally noticed myself, and I did not want ever to go back to that hospital again.

I had finally understood what the great NFL coach Tom Landry meant when he said, "Setting a goal is not the main thing. It is deciding how you will go about achieving it and staying with that plan." I needed to decide here and now how I was going to achieve this goal of running a marathon, because I knew that the path I was on might mean serious health issues down the road, and I wasn't looking for that.

As I looked out my front window with my leg extended up on the coffee table, the sun was flitting through the clouds, almost as if it was beckoning me to come outside and run. I so desperately wanted to be out there as I watched a runner pass by with a look of triumph on his face. Being cooped up inside was not for me anymore, and with my free time at home, I decided to write out three goals for myself: 1) hydrate, hydrate, hydrate; 2) eat better, and in doing so, gain some muscle and weight back; and 3) run as fast as I could without crossing the line into injury territory.

As I arrived at my next cardiologist appointment at the University Hospital in London, hobbling with crutches in hand, I found my way to the ultrasound room once again. It was my Kodak moment yet again. As the cardiologist's technician applied the lotion and took pictures of my heart, I couldn't help but ask if everything seemed alright. I was quite amazed that this technician was willing to share all kinds of information about how the heart worked and what he was looking at. As an innocent comment I asked the technician, "Do I need surgery?" I was pleasantly surprised to hear his take on what he saw.

He concurred that I did have heart valve disease, but from his vantage point, although he was not a cardiologist, it didn't look bad. In fact, he labeled my heart valve disease as mild. As I got off the bed, the technician informed me that the cardiologist would be with me in a few short moments, after he viewed both the pictures and videos that were just taken.

As I walked to the waiting room, I couldn't help but marvel at the beauty of what I just saw. This muscle pumps blood around in the body, never once taking a break. The blood it pumps carries oxygen and nutrients around the body and delivers it to the different organs and tissues. The blood then removes waste products from the tissues, keeping everything working in perfect union. God had created something beautiful. Life itself is dependent on the efficient operation of the heart.

At that moment, the cardiologist called me into his office. As I stood at the door, I couldn't help but gasp. He had wall-to-wall TV screens, and I saw and heard my heart on all the monitors, all in surround sound, as well. It was absolutely amazing. The doctor invited me to take a seat, and I asked him if he was supplying the popcorn. As he began explaining to me what he was seeing from the videos that were taken just minutes before, I couldn't help but be mesmerized by watching the blood flow through the chamber of the heart. And then I saw it: the leaky valve. As the cardiologist pointed to the leaky valve, my heart leapt for joy when he said, you have a mild form of heart disease, and you don't need surgery.

"Can I keep running?" I asked before the doctor could take his next breath.

"I cannot see why not," he said. "It would definitely strengthen your heart. As soon as your leg gets better, you can start running."

That was the best news I had heard all weekend, as I quickly grabbed my crutches and began a slow hobble down the hall. I was ready to begin running, and I was going to start today.

As I got home, I was overjoyed. I knew it was going to turn out well. My wife had informed me that the orthopedic surgeon wanted to see me that afternoon. So with my running attire on and running shoes laced up, I made my way over to see the very doctor who would give me the run-down on the damage I had done to my knee.

As I limped into the doctor's office, I was amazed to see how many people were there who were much worse than I was. I was indeed fortunate, because so many individuals in that waiting room could hardly walk. I was by no means the youngest person there; the age range went from a newborn to the elderly. I was called in immediately.

As the doctor approached me, he saw that I had running attire on and couldn't help but ask how I did in The Bridge Race. I told him that even though I had a few minutes of sleeping time on the asphalt, I finished the race in the 66th spot.

"That-a-boy," he said, as he held his chart over my knee. "I got some good news for you. We can do surgery for you, but you really don't need it. It will heal faster with a little rest, exercise, and a good knee brace, and you will be good as gold." That was all I needed to hear, and I was ready to start my running career again.

The day was going extremely well for me, until I got home. As I walked back into my home, my wife informed me that the cardiologist in Sarnia wanted to see me again.

I was starting to get "doctored out." I thought these doctors had added my number on their speed dial. I was getting more calls from members of the medical profession than I was from telemarketers. I was really getting my exercise going from place to place. Training for the marathon had started, and I hadn't even realized it. I was almost certain these back-and-forth visits were going to kill me.

I made my way back to the original cardiologist who had initially sent me to London for a second opinion. I knew he was about to share the news that I didn't need surgery. I wondered, as I walked into his office, why he just didn't tell me that over the phone. I knew that this cardiologist had labeled my heart valve disease as moderate-to–severe, and the cardiologist in London had said it was mild, so I was just imagining what he was about to tell me next.

The cardiologist explained that he had just gotten off the phone with the other cardiologist in London, and they have both agreed that I need to see another cardiologist to get one more opinion. Their verdict was split. One cardiologist still wanted surgery that other said was not necessary.

Oh my, I thought, as the doctor went on to explain that another cardiologist was coming down from Toronto University Hospital to look at the evidence. This doctor was the leading doctor in the area of heart valve disease, and he would be the one to determine whether or not I needed surgery.

Just when I thought we were almost done, another appointment. My life was filled with appointments. I had no time for anything else. It was becoming all consuming. Then it hit me. This was my heart, and I wanted the best. I needed to quit my whining. I was blessed to have great doctors who were concerned, not only for my well-being, but who wanted only the best for me. What was even more amazing was that it just so happened that this doctor from Toronto was flying to Sarnia the very next day, and he would be able to give us the verdict then. The final verdict would come from him. The good news about this process was that I didn't need to go for any further testing. They had all the pictures and videos they needed to make an educated diagnosis. Regardless of the outcome, I knew God had a plan for me, and I was in God's hands. I just had to believe.

I had known this as a young boy growing up in a rural area. I attended a small elementary school in the middle of nowhere, and it was there I had seen God's plan for my life. I was never an athletic person, but I had a teacher in that school who inspired me to believe in myself and said that I could do anything I wanted. His name was Jim Douglas, and Jim did something for me I never forgot: he believed in me. Mr.

Douglas was a Christian, and he was not afraid to stand up for his beliefs. He was our grade eight teacher, and he was not only fair and compassionate, but he was also the disciplinary teacher. You did not want to cross Mr. Douglas. Everyone knew his expectations, and if you chose to disobey them, then there were consequences. Sometimes very serious consequences, called "the strap."

As a young boy, Mr. Douglas inspired me to run for the cross-country team, and I did. He was always there at the meets, cheering me on, and I remember that, as I was running those races, I never wanted to let him down. I was going to do my best for him. Little would I know that his encouragement would plant that seed which would inspire me to run the greatest race in the world, the Boston Marathon.

In grade eight, I was not an over-achieving academic student, but Mr. Douglas encouraged me to do my best. In fact, that year I failed a number of subjects in his class, but he moved me on to high school, in the academic stream, because he believed in me. Something I would cherish for a lifetime.

As I entered high school, I did not play many sports until my later years. I did play on the soccer team for a few years, but it wasn't until I got to grade thirteen when I would join the school's track and badminton team. I joined only because there were some good-looking girls on the team, and it was about time that I had them notice me, and the best way to do that was join a team.

In high school, I got along with everyone, and everyone got along with me. I had no time for judging people, but rather found myself talking to anyone who would listen to me. And then it happened!

Spring had arrived, and the birds and the bees had begun to signal that it was prom time. The yearly tradition of nominating a prom king and queen was about to begin. As fate would have it, my name was nominated. There were many nominations, and the high school staff was to select the top five individuals they believe would best represent the school in the prom. The rest of the student body would then vote from one of the selected five for their king and queen. And once again, I was honored to have been chosen one of the five. Now the tough part came. It was now time to leave a lasting impression upon the student body as to who I was and why they needed to vote for me.

So I did what came naturally. I started handing out food, particularly candy, to everyone who came by me. In fact, I went through bags and bags of suckers. I thought the best way to win a vote was through their stomachs, and I was right. When prom night came, there was lots of excitement in the air. The new prom king and queen results were going to be unveiled at midnight, and someone would hold a new reign. As the results were read, I stood there in utter disbelief when I heard that over 96-percent of the school body had voted for this one prom king, something that had never been done before in the school's history. The audience was now hushed as a few balloons fell to the ground in anticipation of the announcement. As I thought upon hearing that 96-percent, I then heard it as the master of ceremonies said, "Your new prom king will be …Wes Harding."

The balloons fell from the heavens as it rained confetti all over the crowd. There was much cheering and clapping as I took the throne. It was a moment that literally instilled in me to dream big and that anything was possible.

As I entered university that fall, the crowds were much larger, and no one had heard of prom king Wes Harding nor had they cared to. To make your mark on this world is hard. I guess if it were easy, everybody would be doing it. I had to once again blaze my own trail in this school, except little did I know that this trail would take some paradoxical thinking. I would need to be creative and look at problems a different way than most people.

I attended McMaster University in Hamilton, Ontario. My dream was to get a four-year Honors Bachelor of Arts degree. Upon entering this university, I had to take a writing competence test. It was an hour-long test that consisted of multiple-choice literacy questions, such as spelling, grammar, and paragraph and sentence structure. Anything that had to do with English, was on this test. The rule was that you had to pass this test by the end of the second year of university. If you did not pass it, you were not granted acceptance back into the university. The university felt that if you could not pass by the second year, then you weren't competent enough to meet the requirements and to move on to years three and four.

English has never been my favorite subject, so after that first year at university, I had failed all the attempts to pass this multiple-choice exam. Upon entering my second year, I received a warning from the university stating I must pass this writing competency test by the end of that year, or I would not be eligible to return for my third year. I was in danger of losing not just one year of tuition and the cost of residence, but two years. So I was determined more than ever to pass this test.

All attempts to pass this test proved futile in my second year, and I knew I was in trouble. I then did something uncharacteristic of me. I gambled on the fact that the school really didn't know me, since I was one of thousands of students in this school, and the office of the registrar's computer systems would just recognized my student number and the number of courses I had successfully completed. I had bet that their computer systems would flag me out if I had passed all my subjects in the second year and not passed the test. However, if I failed one subject, I technically had not completed all the required courses for second year, and their computer systems would not flag me out. So with this in mind, I neglected to write the final exam in one of my courses. With me not writing this exam, I would end up failing this one course, and hence, not meeting the required number of credits needed to end the second year of study.

As the end of the second year came to a close, I received a welcoming letter from the University stating that they were welcoming me back for my third year. To meet the credit number for graduation that year, I needed to complete one extra course over and above my regular course load to meet the requirements for third year! *I knew it would work*, I thought to myself. I just gained myself one more year to pass this test. This would at least get me a B.A. in my course of study, even though I was looking for a fourth year's Honors B.A. degree. But I thought I would worry about that later. I had one more year to pass this test.

All attempts to pass the writing test failed during my third year. I passed all my courses, even the extra course I took. I knew the university's computer system would flag me, now, as not passing my writing test as required by ending the second year.

It would only be hours later I would receive a letter by registered mail, requesting me to meet with the dean of studies. I knew the handwriting was on the wall for me. I should have never gotten to the third year like I did, but it worked.

My heart was beating like a drum, as I felt as though this was a death march, walking into his impressive office and meeting this distinguished educator. As a young naive student, I felt intimidated to meet this educated professor. I sat across from him, overlooking the top of his old wooden desk, and I knew what he was thinking about as he looked at me with his glaring eyes.

His first question out of his mouth was, "So, how did you do it?"

Playing a little dumb, I said, "Do what?"

A smile came over his face, as we both knew what he was talking about. A smile came over mine as I said to him that, since the writing competency test was both new for the students and university that first year I arrived, I banked on the fact the university still hadn't worked out all the scenarios as to flagging students out of their computer system who hadn't passed their test by second year. In theory, I explained, I hadn't completed my entire workload of courses required to pass second year, but I was missing one. That allowed me to go back into university in my third year, unnoticed by anyone. I took all the required courses for the third, plus the one extra course that I failed in the second year, to meet the requirement of graduating with a B.A. It wasn't until I finished the requirements for the third year that the computer system flagged me. The computer flagged me, all right, but it was too late. I had earned my degree. Even though I had not passed the writing test I had met the requirements of the university to graduate with a B.A.

The dean of the university did something I was not expecting. He stood up and shook my hand. This experience was new for the university, and they had figured out every scenario but that one.

The dean looked at me and asked me an unusual question. "I am not a betting man," he said, "but I am willing to let you back into this university and let you get your honors degree as a fourth-year student, if you are willing to take a fourth-year-level English writing course at the local community college."

I was so excited I told him that I was willing to take that course, but he wasn't finished with his sentence.

"Here is where the gamble comes in," said the dean. "For you to graduate from our school, you must get 100-percent in this fourth-year English writing course that only English majors and journalists take. If you don't, then you can still graduate from our school. However, your transcript will be inscribed with a sentence that says, 'This student has not passed the McMaster Test of Writing Competence.' With that inscription, it will be very difficult for you to get a job anywhere."

I thought about his offer, and in my excitement, I said I would take it. And so, it was agreed upon. As I left his office, I knew what he was thinking: *This guy is not going to do it.* And I was thinking, *This guy is going to do it. It will probably kill me doing this, but I know I can do this.*

The passing of the writing competence test was now over for me. No longer would I have to take this test, ever again, but I had to prove that I was capable of using English proficiently. If 100-percent is what the dean wanted, then 100-percent he would get.

As the year progressed, my workload was at an all-time high. Figuratively speaking, it was killing me. All my energy was being put into this one course, but with a full course-load and thesis to complete on top, I often thought to myself, *What doesn't kill you makes you stronger.* And so the stronger I got. Hours and hours of writing and studying brought me down to this one assignment. I would need to complete a thirty-page writing assignment for my college English course. I was heading into this final assignment with a one hundred, something that very few students could ever achieve. I so desperately needed a 100-percent on this paper.

As I pondered what I would write this paper on, it hit me. I would write a paper on why the McMaster test of writing competence was not a reliable test; why this test was not a true indicator of a student's writing ability. If I could prove this test was not doing what it was intended to do, then my paper would make headlines around the community. So to the university archives I went, in search of how this test was initially designed and developed. Hours would be spent looking through documents and notes. My paper was now complete. Thirty-plus pages were put together to illustrate that the McMaster test of writing competence was an incompetent test to begin with. It was flawed, and I had proved my point in this essay.

As I submitted this paper to my college English professor, he smiled, and said that he was looking forward to reading this paper. My life hung in the balance but regardless of the mark, I had done my best. There were no short cuts, no excuses, just countless hours of effort and a lot of ink.

As the papers were handed back a week later, my heart leaped with joy as the professor came up to me and said, "You've done it! You got your 100-percent."

I was overjoyed. The long hours and hard work had once again proven to me that you will always reap what you sow. I was looking forward to giving the dean at the university this paper and having him read my findings, not to show him I won, but to improve the education system.

As I walked into the office of the Dean of Studies at the university, his smile said it all, and he said, "You've done it. You have definitely proven your point. Well done." He shook my hand and said, "We will read your paper and seriously consider your results and recommendations for us. Thank you."

It would not be until months later, after graduating from McMaster University that I would find out that whenever the university would mention the McMaster Test of writing competence on any of its documents, it would have an asterisk placed beside it that stated, "This regulation is currently under review."

***

As I looked back on those defining moments in my life, it has once again reminded me that it is possible to do the impossible. These milestones have taught me to push the limits, try new things, and go outside my comfort zones. Your mind will never know how far you can go until you try. Never let anyone tell you it is impossible. Muhammad Ali said, "Impossible is just a big word thrown around by small men who find it easier to live in the world they've been given than to explore the power they have to change it. Impossible is not a fact. It's an opinion. Impossible is not a declaration. It's a dare. Impossible is potential. Impossible is temporary. Impossible is nothing."

The hour had now come to find out what the final verdict would be from this cardiologist from Toronto. As I went to meet with him, I was pleasantly surprised to see my original cardiologist from Sarnia, instead. The doctor told me that the cardiologist from Toronto had spent about an hour on my file, and the results were simple. No operation needed. It didn't matter that my heart valve disease was mild, or moderated-to-severe, they would just keep observing and testing me year to year. At this point in time, no surgery would be needed, since I have had this since birth. He continued to explain that I would need to perform yearly stress tests and no medication would be necessary. His final statement was chilling, as he said, "You are a lucky man to have this collapse happen to you. Very rarely do we ever detect heart valve disease in patients until they are dead. Keep running as you chase after the wind. I will see you one year from now."

I guess God did know best. A bad thing turned out to be a great blessing in disguise for me. It was true what doesn't kill does make you stronger. It was now time for me to chase after my dream: run a marathon.

Marathon number one, here I come!

MILE 110

The Prize Is Waiting For Me

> *"God has given me the ability. The rest is up to me!"*

The summer sun was inviting me to come outside and run. I had now been laid up for three weeks with my leg in a knee brace. My running shoes were beckoning me to warm my feet in their form-fitting embrace. The thrill of the run was about to begin, as I hobbled out the front door. My goal was to run to the end of the block, turn around, and come back. I was a little hesitant in doing this, and I heard my wife say as I went out the front door, "Are you sure you want to do this? You could do more damage now by pushing yourself too soon. You haven't given yourself enough time to heal."

My wife was always right, I knew. But I was an old, stubborn mule, and I couldn't help but be enticed by the outdoors. I reasoned that the human body was made to move, and I was getting tired sitting on the couch for so long. Considering I had only been running for a year and a half, my couch was no longer my friend. My running shoes were, and I just had to try them out. As I closed the front door, my mind was now in running mode and the thought of damaging my knee more was a distant concern. I would go slowly, I convinced myself. I wasn't planning on winning any races that day. So with a slight limp and my MP3 player on, I jumped on the next gust of wind and was on my way, shuffling down the sidewalk.

I must have looked really strange running with a twist and a hop because as I went by my neighbors, the look on their faces as they peered through the curtains said it all. This guy is crazy. As I neared the end of the block I felt good, almost too good. I slowly turned around and made my way back, trying to run a negative split in doing so. It felt so good to be out running on the streets again.

I knew in my heart at that very moment, I was destined to run.

God had performed a miracle, and there was nothing stopping me now. He has given me this ability to run, and I wanted to use it to glorify Him. Although I knew I still had a long ways to go to reach Boston, I was determined to make this happen. As I arrived home, my cheerleaders were waiting for me. It was as if I had won my first race. They were excited to see in my eyes that my dream was alive again.

That afternoon, I set my next goal. I was going to run my first marathon. Even though the dog days of summer were upon us, I signed up for a fall marathon that was to be held in Toronto, Ontario. It was called the Scotiabank Marathon, and it was a Boston qualifier. It was the beginning of July, and the marathon was to be run during the last weekend of September. That meant I had twelve weeks of training to prepare for this marathon. Of those twelve weeks, I knew I probably only had eight solid weeks of training. But I knew anything was possible, and I was willing to give it a try!

As the summer progressed along, my leg got better, and I was improving in both my speed and distance each week. Although I needed to wear a knee brace when I ran, I still experienced pain. Pain was my constant companion, but I never felt more alive than getting out on the open road and feeling every part of my body scream out to me that this was too hard. Even though I struggled to push through the insurmountable odds of meeting the requirements to qualify for Boston, I still had to do my part. God had done His part by giving me that desire and my health back to run. To do my part, I was back running again, and I needed to put in the long hours to fulfill my responsibility in seeing this dream come true.

When the marathon weekend came, my family and I packed our bags and set off to the big city. As we arrived in Toronto for our first big race, we knew within our hearts it was not going to be our last. With cameras in hand, my daughters were ready to announce to the world that their father was debuting in his first ever marathon.

The date, September 27, 2009, would be forever etched in my mind as I lined up with over 1,000 runners who were just as anxious as I was to begin the race. The crowds were electrifying. I thought it would not be in my best interest to start near the front of the race with the Africans, so I started in the middle of the pack. I rationalized this by saying that there was no greater feeling than passing people. The warm, humid conditions that day brought on a little drizzle to cool down the runners, as the morning temperatures began to rise.

This was my first marathon race, and I was about to blaze a trail to Boston with my enthusiasm and determination. As the gun sounded to start the race, my legs were fresh with energy. I sprinted down the straightaway, passing hundreds of runners. *This is my moment,* I thought. Although I had never run any more than 32 kilometers leading up to this race, I felt as though I could run 100 kilometers. This was going to be a good day.

I looked down on my watch as I passed the 10-kilometer marker; I was projected to meet the qualifying time for Boston. As a forty-two-year-old male, my qualifying time to run Boston was 3:20:00. I knew to accomplish this time would require my undivided attention to my pace time, and I knew after my last experience that I needed to be hydrated properly throughout the race.

There was no greater feeling than seeing the 10-kilometer marker; one quarter of the race had been completed. As I looked up from my watch, I saw the Africans coming up the other side of the street. Their style and form of running was as graceful as a deer running across the fields. I was amazed at their speed and endurance, as I realized they had just completed 16 kilometers when I had just finished my tenth. But that didn't matter. After witnessing the greatest runners in the world, I was energized to continue my pace and stay focused to my game plan.

As I crossed the half-way point, I looked at my watch and was pleased with what I had seen and accomplished thus far. With only 21.1 kilometers left, the crowds were thinning out, and we were set to run alone. Just us and the open road. We were all running for the prize that awaited us…and then I felt it.

It was that twinge in my leg that I had recognized just a few months ago. I knew the pain that was about to follow it. In my haste, I realized I was not taking enough water throughout the race. I was wearing a special knee brace, but I knew from each step that brace was doing everything it could to keep my knee in place.

Onward I labored, until the 24-kilometer mark. With each stride I was taking I was growing increasingly weary and as I looked at my watch I knew my qualifying time was in jeopardy. I began to stagger and weave a bit on the road. I had a flashback moment as I remembered the time when I had collapsed in my last 10-kilometer race. I knew I had an important decision to make at that time, a decision that would change my course of action for the rest of the race. Would I continue to push through the pain in hopes of making it to the finish line in qualifying time? The risk was high. I could seriously injury myself eliminating me from running for months or worse yet permanently injuring myself. Or would I slow down, finish the race, and live to run another day. The decision was now paramount.

I pondered my outcome for a few moments and came to realize that I came to finish my first marathon, not to be taken home in an ambulance. Just over a year ago, this feat of running a marathon was just a dream. Now it had become a reality. The goal of reaching Boston would have been nice, but I knew it wasn't meant to be that day. My disappointment turned to excitement as I started walking to regain my composure and enjoy the scenery as I jog slowly by some beautiful monuments in Toronto. I wanted to finish my race, and although running the Boston was not going to happen, the greatest thrill was completing what I had set at to do: finish my first marathon.

The old marathon saying goes, as you hit the 32-kilometer marker (20 miles) you still have the second half of the race to run. Marathon runners typically hit the wall at this point. In endurance sports, such as running or cycling, *hitting the wall* refers to the fact that you have depleted all your glycogen (stored energy) stored in the liver and muscles, which manifests itself through a loss of energy and fatigue. Runners start to slow down at this point, even to the point of walking. Severe muscle cramps can begin, which makes the last 10 kilometers seem like a very long way. The key for marathon runners in training is to continually be pushing the wall back. Marathon runners do this by progressively going out for longer runs each week during their training period, and in doing so, the body's capacity to store more glycogen within your muscles increases. By increasing your glycogen levels, you are able to maintain your pace and hopefully push off the onset of fatigue.

As I hit the 32-kilometer mark, I found myself enjoying the race. With each passing step, I started to experience the runners high. Almost like an oxymoron, I was in pain, but I was enjoying every minute of it. It was as if I was entering into a runner's nirvana, a very peaceful and blissful state. And then I saw it, or rather heard it, first. The finishing line was nearing as the crowds got louder from excitement. I could taste victory; I could see my dream being accomplished. There was no greater feeling running down the home stretch to the cheers of thousands of spectators. I was looking for my family, but I also knew they were looking for me. As I crossed the finish line with a time of 3:43:58, I had done it. I had placed in 571st spot. It was a proud moment as my family gathered around me and gave the biggest hugs a father could ever get. Those hugs were a confirmation from the angels above that the dream was achieved.

I look back on that race and even though I was 23 minutes slower than what I needed to qualify for Boston, it didn't matter. I would live to run another day. With all the walking I had done in that marathon I knew I could improve with more training. This was the day the Lord had made I rejoiced in it.

Over the years, I have come to the realization that fulfillment of one's personal goals is better than winning a prize for first place. Fulfilling a goal provides an inner satisfaction that comes from knowing that you have worked hard to achieve something, and the good feeling that comes from that is better than any hardware one could ever receive.

When I got home that night, I said to my wife that my dreaming was not over yet. I told her I wanted to go back to university in the following fall and get another degree. That meant I would have to take an unpaid sabbatical from my teaching position and trust in the Lord to provide the necessary income to provide, not only for my expenses at school but also for my family at home. I knew God had given me the ability to learn, and I wanted to do my part and use it. The question once again came down to, if we knew that this was God's plan for our lives, could we trust Him to once again provide everything we needed for that one year.

The answer for us was a no-brainer. God had proven Himself to us on numerous occasions, and we did not want to miss out on His blessing. So that fall, the dream continued. I enrolled at the University of Windsor in anticipation of getting my Bachelors of Education degree. Education has been an ever-changing profession, and I wanted to keep current as the winds of change kept blowing through our province. I wanted to become the best teacher I could for my students. I knew there would be sacrifices to make, and I also knew that I would have to put in long hours of studying and writing reports, but I was no stranger to hard work. It could be done. The dream of running could continue while I studied at university, and this brought on a whole new outlook for me. It was fun living the dream, and I was about to live dream number two. Very few people are blessed to live out one dream in their lifetime, but to live out two dreams is a rarity. How much more can a person be blessed by God?

As the onset of winter began, I started training to run my second marathon. The next marathon I chose would be run in our nation's capital, Ottawa, Ontario. It would be a spring marathon, and I was determined that this would be my race to run the time I needed to qualify for Boston. Ottawa is a beautiful city, the very city in which our country's prime minister resides. This race would prove to be very exciting, as we would be running right past the home of our prime minister. The beauty of the scenery that Ottawa offered would be a runner's delight. This race would be run just months before I headed off to university to live out dream number two.

As the spring breeze blew, the flowers were in their best display for the nation's annual marathon. I had once again trained all winter long, determined to improve in both my time and finishing place. This race had attracted runners from all over the world. It was destined to be the country's best marathon race, and I didn't want to miss it. I wanted this race, and this race wanted me to qualify for Boston. Leading up to this race, I had trained harder, eaten better, and I just knew it was going to be my day.

As always, my biggest encouragers, my family, packed their bags and together we set sail for a distant place. A place that would lead to the horizon called "where dreams were made of." The car seemed to float as we made the eight-hour trek to Ottawa, Ontario.

It was race time once again, and with tens of thousands of spectators and runners in the nation's capital, you couldn't help but feel the excitement in the air. The flowers took their stand along the road in full bloom as we ventured to the starting line. With a population of just over a million people, the city ranks as the cleanest in Canada and third in the world. With the clean, crisp air welcoming runners to begin a journey of 42 kilometers around the city, I couldn't help but notice some Kenyan runners jogging just under our hotel room, waiting in anticipation of the big race. I motioned to the girls to get their cameras as I burst out of the hotel room and caught up with the elite runners from Kenya. I knew that, since I couldn't beat them in the marathon, I decided to join them. As they jogged down the street, so did I, shoulder to shoulder, and I thought to myself, *So this is what it is like to run with a Kenyan.* One day, I knew I would be running with the world's best Africans in one of the world's best races, Boston, and this was my day.

Like a good and prepared runner, I took a quick inventory ensuring that I had everything I needed for this race. Nothing was going to hold me back. I did not want the Boston experience to elude me like it did in the last marathon. With my fuel belt on, I was ready to begin. I knew, as Bill Rogers had once said, "A marathon can humble you," so I was determined not to sprint out of the gates setting a blazing trail in the first few kilometers. It would require willpower to keep at a steady, constant pace, but for me, like most runners, this is difficult. With adrenaline flowing through the veins, it is hard not to sprint the first few kilometers, but it is *runner beware* in doing so, because later on in the race, the marathon will certainly humble you.

As we lined up in our projected finishing lines, it was announced that our prime minister would be just outside his home cheering for us. Race officials encouraged us to wave, smile, cheer anything we could to let the prime minister know we were experiencing a thrill of a lifetime. I was prepared to make the most of this opportunity. *Wes Harding is going to be seen and not forgotten by the prime minister as he makes his way by his house,* I thought as the gun sounded.

The weather was once again humid as we ran through the streets of Ottawa. My Garmin watch had become my friend in my training days and was my source of encouragement along the journey. As I zoned in, I was oblivious to my surroundings. As I rounded one of the street corners, I happened to look up at the street sign. It read *Sussex Drive.* In my horror of horrors, I realized in my zoned-in state, I missed seeing the prime minister of Canada. I looked back down the street and noticed a rather large crowd waving and cheering as they went by the home of the prime minister of Canada…and I missed it. I looked at my watch, it was too late, there would be no turning back to see the prime minister. I had another appointment waiting for me, and it was Boston.

Once again, at the half-way mark, I felt good. I was doing everything possible to keep my pace constant. I knew qualifying was within my grasp as I headed towards the wall that awaited me. This time, I brought my Gatorade and energy gel to help me go around the wall. Then it happened. At the 35-kilometer mark, I could smell the roses that bloomed by the finish line. Another 7 kilometers and I was finished, and my time would be good enough to qualify for Boston. But this time something happened I wasn't prepared for. In my haste to meet the target pace, I ended up with a severe muscle cramp at the back of my thigh. This pain was so intense and paralyzing I could barely stand on it. As each second passed by, I felt my hope of achieving the qualifying time disappear. I was determined to finish the race, but was really disappointed in knowing this was neither the time nor the place I would fulfill my dream.

As I continued to hobble the remainder of the distance, I had wondered why God had allowed this, but then I realized I wasn't doing my part. In my haste, I knew that this could have been prevented by adequately hydrating and fueling my body with nutrition that it desperately needed. I had run out of supplies on my fuel belt at the 32-kilometer mark, but I thought I had enough in me to finish. It wasn't meant to be as I crossed the finish line in 3:28:35. Just over 8 minutes slower than what I needed to qualify. I was coming so close, but still I was so far away.

As I met my family, once again their cheering and hugs encouraged me not to give up on my dream. I knew I could do it. It just meant another six months of training. But first, dream number two was waiting for me.

In September of that year, I went back to school. I had been out of school for twenty years, and I realized a lot had changed since I had been there last. New faces, new teachers, new textbooks, but that didn't matter, change is good. On the first day of school, my first destination was to the gym, since I knew between courses I could devote my extra time to training. I was overjoyed when I walked into the gymnasium to see an indoor track. It was my dream come true. I could train indoors all winter longs. It was beautiful. I would have never thought during my days as a couch potato that I would be saying that indoor tracks were beautiful, but I had changed now, and that was a good thing.

With my dream of going back to school starting, I fixed my focus on qualifying for Boston. So I signed up for a fall marathon in Niagara Falls, Ontario. Its claim to fame is that it is "the most famous finish line in the world." Nestled beside the Horseshoe Falls, runners crossing the finish line are welcomed by the thunderous roar of the falls. It is the one marathon in North American where you begin in one country and finish in another, and I was ready to take it on.

Once again, the thrill of chasing the dream was ahead of me as I stood on the starting line of the marathon in Buffalo, New York. This day was different. This day, the sun was shining and, with the wind at my back, it was going to be a glorious day. The trees that lined the streets were all dressed in their majestic colors. The slight breeze that blew through the trees warned us that the temperature was getting warmer. With the right amount of hydration and nutrition, I raced on toward the prize. The race was better than expected, but as fate would have it, at the

40-kilometer mark, with only 2 kilometers left, a severe muscle cramp at the back of my leg would visit me, wanting me to stop and tend to its calling.

I still had time, with 1 kilometer left, to meet the qualify time of 3:20:00. So with every hop, skip, and jump I took, I tried with all my might to reach the finish line. As I looked at the official clock as I crossed the line, it read 3:22:22. Just 2 minutes shy of making the mark. Disappointment of not meeting the time was replaced with the realization I was getting faster, and I was determined to not let this dream get away. That afternoon upon returning from home, I signed up for my fourth marathon. This one would be held in the spring of 2011, in the city of Waterloo, Ontario. The cold Canadian winter would once again be my friend, as I was going to train like never before.

That winter, we experienced snow like we had never seen it before. It would go down as one of the worst and coldest winters on record. I have always said that I was born on the wrong continent, as I am not a winter person at all. The cold, ice, sleet, and snow are not my idea of a good time.

That December, my father was having a serious head operation at the university hospital in London, Ontario. He had suffered for many years from trigeminal neuralgia, also known as the suicide disease, because people often commit suicide because of its severe pain before an operation could happen. Operations of this magnitude take years to plan and prepare for.

Trigeminal neuralgia is a nerve disorder that causes stabbing or electric-shock-like pain in parts of the face. The pain of trigeminal neuralgia comes from the trigeminal nerve. This nerve carries the feelings of touch and pain from the face, eyes, sinuses, and mouth to the brain. A serious operation would be needed. My father's major artery to his brain had wrapped around the trigeminal nerve, causing severe pain that would often paralyze my father from doing anything until the pain had subsided. The doctors would have to drill through the back of my father's skull, unwrap the artery that had tangled itself around the trigeminal nerve in the front of his face, and put a pad around it to prevent the trigeminal nerve from touching the artery. The operation would take seven hours, with seven surgeons and many nurses in attendance, to correct the situation.

The operation was set for six in the morning on Monday, December 13, 2011. For my father to arrive in London at this time, I had arranged to take him to the hospital. It would take us an hour to arrive at the hospital, so we decided to leave at four in the morning. This would leave him an hour to sign in and prepare for an operation that could potentially end his life.

That night before the operation, we experienced the largest snowstorm we had ever received. Blowing and drifting snow, whiteouts were everywhere. The police were warning travelers to stay off the roads, and they had even closed down the roads due to the dangerous condition. Knowing that I could potentially be hindered by elements, I left an hour earlier to pick up my father and make our way to London. Snow, ice, and closed roads could not hold me back from getting my father to the hospital for this ever-so-important operation.

The road conditions were treacherous. The snowplows had been pulled off the road, and it was just us and the unrelenting blowing snow. The drive was slow and laborious. Oftentimes, we wondered if God would get us through the storm so that my father could have this ever so important operation. To reschedule this appointment would take months or possibly years. We had to get there. There was no other option. We often felt the Lord guiding our vehicle through snowdrifts that were begging us not to go through. We could hear the wind telling us to turn around and go home. But we would not heed the winds' or the snow's warning; there would be no turning around. We would not take no for an answer.

As we arrived at the front doors of the hospital, it was one minute till six. The Lord had done the impossible. It took us three hours to drive

100 kilometers, but we did it. My father was now in the Lord's hands. As I watched him go through the hospital doors, I said a quick prayer to God, knowing that could be the last time I would ever see him.

With my father in the hospital, it was now time to turn around and head home. I needed to get back to the family business and take the place of my father in his absence. The drive back along the main highway was uneventful. The roads were snowy but drivable. I was now only 20 kilometers from home, and then it happened. The traffic on the highway came to a complete stop. As far as the eye could see ahead, cars lined the highway. Maybe it was an accident that had us come to a complete stop, or maybe it was a slow moving snowplow. Whatever the reason, we waited. After several hours of waiting, people started getting out of their cars and walking up and down the side of the highway. People began visiting with one another, speculating as to what was happening. No news reports were given on the radio as to any accidents that had happened. Nor was there any mention of us waiting on the highway for several hours. It was as if we did not even exist.

The day's work at the family business had been wasted, as I just sat in my vehicle. I was becoming impatient, as I needed to be back at the university three hours away to write two exams for the following day. As a restless runner, I needed to get out and stretch my legs.

As I got out of my vehicle, I noticed the driver behind me had a Boston 26.2 sticker on his vehicle. This driver had noticed my 26.2 sticker as well, and immediately a bond was formed between the two of us. We had something in common, something to talk about to pass the time. He informed me that he was a doctor on his way to perform an operation at the hospital in Sarnia. As an accomplished marathon runner, he shared with me some running strategies on nutrition and hydration for achieving my goal of qualifying for Boston. As he shared some invaluable bits of information, I immediately thought that God had placed one of his angels behind my vehicle to open my eyes and encourage me not to give up on the dream. As we stood there shoulder-to-shoulder on that highway, I thanked the Lord for stopping me and encouraging me to keep going.

As evening came and the gales of December blew upon us, the snowstorm turned for the worse. People on the highway were now becoming impatient, as no news had been given to us as to why we had come to a complete stop on a major highway. It looked like we were destined to spend the night in our vehicles. The drifts were forming around the cars, and people were starting to run out of gas. We knew that the people in the vehicles beside us were going to be our neighbors. The temperature dropped to -20 Celsius, and the darkness embraced us with its tight grip of aloneness and abandonment.

It was now over fourteen hours since we had last moved, and there was no hope of being rescued. We were stranded. With no food and no water, people started sharing whatever they had with others. These strangers around us had become our friends, doing and sharing everything they had just to survive. The only comforting news now being offered on the radio was to stay in our vehicles. The entire city had been shut down, and there was no place to go. Even emergency personnel had turned their vehicles in for snowmobiles. It was obvious that we were alone, and we needed each other as we fought the snowstorm of the century.

As I reclined back on my seat in my vehicle, trying in vain to keep warm, I pondered as to why God had placed me on that highway, just to sit here for hours with nothing to do, especially when I had places to go, people to see, and things to do. Sitting in my car in a snowstorm was not where I wanted to be. Then, it was as if God said through an inner voice, "Remember. Remember what you have just heard. It will help you in your pursuit of the dream."

When morning came, those stranded on the highway had become the attention of national news. The storm was still so fierce that snow plows were still unable to start clearing the road. With just over 300 vehicles stuck on Highway 402, we were left in a desperate situation.

With the snow piled high all around the vehicles, people's lives were in danger. No food or water had been provided, and we were left to fend for ourselves. News stations around North America had begun to send up their news crews to report on the dire situation. CNN was quick to take aerial shots from their news helicopters to show how fierce the storm had become. The storm was so severe that a state of emergency was issued by the local authorities. The Canadian military was called in to airlift stranded motorists to safely. Two military helicopters and a C-130 Hercules were used in evacuating people from the highway and taking them to nearby shelters.

As the snow continued to blow, I was determined to make it home. I had now been in my vehicle for over twenty-four hours, and I so longed to get home.

I noticed a heavy equipment operator with his backhoe moving slowly through the drifts, and in my desperation, I got out and flagged him down. It was like a gift from heaven as he said to me to follow behind him. He could plow me through to the nearest gas station, since I was just minutes from running out of gas. Hundreds of cars had experienced this fate during the night. As he plowed, I felt as if God's hand was upon my vehicle and sent an angel to get me out. As we dodged the hundreds of cars abandoned on the road, God had provided a way out for me.

It was a moment of celebration as I drove into the gas station. I filled up my vehicle and headed out on the lonely road to get home. With my four–wheel-drive vehicle, it would take me another nine hours to drive 20 kilometers, but I was determined to get through, snowdrift after snowdrift, but I did it. As I arrived home that night, there was no greater feeling than knowing someone was watching out for me. I would spend a total of thirty-four hours in my vehicle, but I knew God had a purpose for me to experience that, and it would not be until spring when I fully realized why He stopped me in my tracks on that highway.

Spring had sprung, and once again, marathon season had begun. I had registered for the Waterloo Marathon, in Waterloo, Ontario, that was to be held at the end of April. With my training complete, I was now ready to attempt the impossible. As race day approached, I found myself preparing mentally how to navigate the pitfalls and dangers that come from running 26.2 miles. I remembered the advice on nutrition from the marathon doctor who was stranded behind my vehicle, and I took his advice to heart. I was ready. I had run three marathons before, and I knew Albert Einstein was correct in saying that, "The only source of knowledge is experience." I knew what to expect as the miles went on, and I was prepared for it now.

As the race started, the roads all seemed to blend in together, until we got to the edge of the city where the countryside welcomed us with open arms. We were free, indeed. As I looked over the barren farmland, it reminded me of the field of dreams, and this was the race to open the door to a whole new world for me. As I ran, I was continually reminded of the words of wisdom from the doctor just months ago, and each time I thought of him, I replenished my body with the much-needed fluids and nutrients.

At the halfway mark, I was feeling as if I had just started the race. With every breath, the country air filled my lungs with new hope and vision. I continued running as I looked at my watch, and I realized that I was now only 3 kilometers from the finish line, and I was ahead of schedule for my qualifying time. The heavens opened up as the rain poured on us, but this rain was different for me. It was showers of blessings that were coming down on me. I could now see the finishing line, and my family was just walking to the finish line to see me finish. The look of surprise and shock on their faces as I passed them said it all. I had done it! As I crossed the finish line, the official time clock read 3:11:27! I had done it! I beat my qualifying time by over 8 minutes. It was my personal best.

Although I could not see it at the time, my time stranded on the highway with the marathon runner was connected to my success in this marathon. It is funny how God places people in our lives that make a difference. They encourage us and brighten our day. This runner did exactly that for me. He left a lasting impression, and I wanted to do the same as I entered the dream called Boston!

It would be in June of that year, two months later, that I would achieve my second dream: graduating from university with a degree in education. It was convocation time, and students dressed in graduation gowns and caps dotted the stadium. Family members and friends had gathered to celebrate something special, something remarkable, an end of a journey that would open the door to new dreams. As my name was called to receive my diploma, an eruption of applause came from the crowd. It was sweet a sound, almost the same sound I had heard when I completed my first dream: crossing the finish line after running a marathon.

Those cheers would confirm to me that it was all worth it. It was just twelve months earlier naysayers came out to extinguish my dream of going back to school by saying that it was not possible. Forty-three-year-olds don't go back to school and live the dream. Today, I proved them wrong. As I approached the president and vice-chancellor of the university, their words of encouragement would make the effort all worthwhile as they said, "Well done, and congratulations. The world awaits you." With my diploma in hand, this certificate would be living proof to me that dreams do come true, and you are never too old to begin.

I learned that day to live each day as if it was my last. When that happens, the world changes, because I have changed. My outlook and perspective changes. If I looked in the mirror every morning and asked myself if this was the last day of my life, would I want to do what I am about to do today? If my answer was no, then I needed to change something.

Life is like a vapor. It appears for a little while, and then it is no more. Our days are numbered, and I was determined to make a lasting impression with the days I had left. The gift of time was given to make the most out of my life . . . so dream number three, get ready.

Next stop, Boston . . . or wait . . . I want to live out another dream, God, before I get to Boston! I want to run with Team Hoyt in the Boston Marathon!

MILE 120

NEXT STOP BOSTON

"It is never too late to be what you might have been."

-George Eliot

I am living the dream, but why did it have to be so hot, I lamented to God, as I looked at my watch through my glossy, bloodshot eyes? My eyes had become a catch basin collecting all the sweat that ran from the top of my head. With each blink I took, I was reminded of the stinging sensation that came from the hot summer days. It was nine o'clock in the morning, and my body's cooling system was already working overtime to combat the heat wave that had rolled in from the south. It was April 16th—a time of year that Bostonians called "springtime," but today was anything but springtime. Today was Patriots Day, the day that signaled the return of the running of the Boston Marathon, and today the "3 Hs" were on tap for the day—hot, hazy, and humid.

The 116th running of the Boston Marathon was soon to begin, and here I was, about to experience my ultimate dream, running in this world-famous race. Just four years ago, I was just on the couch dreaming of this moment, and now I was living it. The only problem was that I didn't realize it was going to be so hot.

For the past forty-eight hours, runners had been receiving weather updates from the Boston Athletic Association (B.A.A.) alerting runners of the pending dangers that would come from running a marathon in the extreme temperatures expect arrive on this particular day on which the Boston Marathon would be run on. The B.A.A. had warned runners that they needed to be alert for signs of heatstroke and dehydration and had asked that those who were inexperienced or ill to skip the race. It was a dire warning urging runners to take extreme caution, which prompted officials to offer a deferment for runners willing to wait until next year to run the race. The alert continued to say that those who trained only in cool climates should consider not running.

As I stood with thousands of runners waiting for the gun to sound at 10 AM to begin the journey to Boston, I had underestimated the stress that the heat would have on the body. I stood in complete stillness, preparing myself mentally for the 26.2 miles that lay ahead. As the sound of helicopters whirled overhead, the talk of the runners was that of doom and gloom. This marathon was going to be a long, hot, grueling run. A run that would challenge even the best of runners.

As I listened to the voices around me, I found we all had something in common: we were strange breed, indeed. Dedicated endurance runners run in all seasons, whether by day or night, hot or cold. Nothing holds us back. For distance runners, the road is to be conquered. Running on the open road becomes our quest to free ourselves from the chains of life. There is freedom in running, a freedom that only runners can understand. Today would be just another run as we nodded in agreement that we didn't come to Boston to watch a race, but rather to finish one.

As the runners waited patiently for the race to begin, the volunteers continued to warn of the impending dangers that lay in wait for us in the miles ahead. Watering stations set up on the starting line had become the popular hangouts for runners, and of course, the talk around the table was the temperature.

Being a newcomer to Boston and unfamiliar with the lay of the land, volunteers told stories of past marathons and how temperatures in Boston can vary from year to year, averaging around 50 degrees. With temperatures being predicted to reach the mid-80s, some 30 degrees above normal, it was doubtful that elite runners would set a new course record this year.

Volunteers not only cautioned that the marathon course would prove challenging, but to mix in that with the blazing sun beating down, it was going to turn into a race for the watering stations. I had pondered this fate for a few moments as I reflected on the fact that it was just forty-eight hours earlier that I was running in Canada with a winter coat, gloves, and hat on, only to come here and peel off every layer possible to keep cool.

I was disappointed in the moment. My heart dropped as I continued to listen to talk around me. The naysayers were out claiming that race times for runners would average 30-60 minutes slower than usual. This was my day to shine, the day for me to set my personal best. I had travelled ten hours to arrive at this very spot, only to be told that my time today would be one of my slowest. How would my friends back home respond when they heard that Boston was my slowest time ever?

As I stood surveying the scene around me, I was reminded that life is sometimes like the weather, unpredictable. Surprises often come our way, and it's how you react to those surprises—good or bad—that determines your outcome. I was determined to make the best of the situation. Although I wanted this marathon to be my personal best time, I knew I had to change my plans. I would have to slow down a little. A smile came over my face as the small, still voice of God assured me that He just wanted my best, and He would do the rest.

As I stepped on the most famous starting line in the world and looked down the straightway, I recalled the time when I had watched the Boston Marathon as a child on TV. The only difference was that this was no longer a dream, but reality. I had to pinch myself to be reminded that dreams do come true and that I was actually here in the flesh. I was no longer a spectator, but a participant, exactly where I wanted to be.

As I glanced to my right, David McGillivray, the race director of the Boston Marathon, was standing right next to me. I was intrigued as I watched him respond with patience to the hundreds of questions runners had about the race. His gentle and reassuring answers gave his audience the confidence and encouragement they needed to run the race to the best of their ability.

With a smile on my face, I walked over to David and I immediately found a common bond between David and myself as we both had something in common in our lives: overcoming obstacles. As David shares in his book, *The Last Pick: The Boston Marathon Race Director's Road to Success*, he too had faced enormous challenges that he had to overcome in his own life. Through his story, he has inspired thousands of people to live the dream. His saying, "If you can dream it, it can happen," inspired me to think beyond Boston, for Boston was just the tip of the iceberg. As we looked at the marathon road ahead, David encouraged me to keep dreaming because "It is never too late to be what you might have been." Today, I was a marathon runner, and I had 26.2 miles ahead of me to think about what I wanted to be tomorrow. This was the exact attitude check I needed. Boston would now be a victory lap for working so hard during the past four years. I was here to enjoy the race and celebrate in God's goodness and faithfulness. This day was God's gift to me. He had made this day, and I was going to rejoice and be glad. The gun was about to be sounded, and I found myself energized as God's still voice said, "Let's run it together!"

I could feel the push of the crowd behind me as we started to move forward, or maybe it was the pull of the runners ahead of us. Either way, we were now on the move! The race had begun, and this was my moment!

As I ran the first 5 kilometers, I found myself soaking in not only the sun's rays, but also the cheers from the spectators. It was an amazing sight. Each step I took reminded me of the thousands of steps I had taken to get me to this time and place. As I began to zone in, I found my mind wandering to the lady in the shoe store, wondering if she was watching the Boston Marathon on TV. But that didn't matter now. Here I was, having this feeling of achieving the impossible. From being told I that would never run a marathon, let alone the Boston Marathon, and now here I was on the road to Boston. It was an amazing feeling of accomplishment!

As the warm summer breeze blew upon us, and like on that first winter night as I ran in a snowstorm, I could once again hear the winds blowing through the branches. It was as if I could hear the applause of the trees again telling me, "Well done. You have done it." But this time those voices and the applause were real, and I looked at the smiling faces of those who lined the streets.

With the heat intensifying, I was determined to stop by every water and aid station along the route. I was glad that the B.A.A. had set up extra water stations along the route to help keep runners hydrated. At that moment, a spectator showered me with his water sprinkler, and with thumbs up, he gave me the much needed encouragement not to give up, but to fight the good fight as the journey continued. I didn't know what the next 37 kilometers would bring, but I was ready for it.

The road had now widened, and the runners around me had started to spread apart. The cheers from the spectators made me smile as they shouted, "You are my hero." As I thought of that statement, I found myself zoning in on my fourth dream, running the Boston Marathon with Team Hoyt, my heroes.

After qualifying for Boston, I was determined to never stop dreaming. So in the months leading up to Boston, I found myself wanting to run the Boston Marathon with Dick and Rick Hoyt. I had known that every year Dick and Rick Hoyt put together a special team called Team Hoyt to represent the Hoyt Foundation in the Boston Marathon. The only problem I had with this dream was, how was I going to fulfill it?

The solution came easy as I remembered the effort I put into completing my first marathon. It would take determination, perseverance and faith. God had brought me this far in my journey, so why not ask Him? At that moment, I recalled the words of Jesus as written in the book of Matthew, in which He said, "Ask and it will be given to you; seek and you will find; knock and the door will be open to you." Was it that easy? Could I be so bold and ask Him for this request? I knew if it was God's will for me to do this, then He would open the doors for me to be on this team. So I asked God, then I made a call to Team Hoyt. If it was meant to be, then I knew it would happen. If not, that was fine with me, and I know God had another plan for me.

As I picked up the phone, my hand shook with excitement. With each ring I felt my heart shake, until I heard her voice. Her name was Kathy, and she was the Team Hoyt office manager. I could not believe that I was actually talking to someone associated with Team Hoyt. I felt like a screaming teenage girl at a pop concert as her idol sang her favorite song. In my excited enthusiasm, I introduced myself and told her a little bit of my journey the past four years of my life. As I shared my dream of being a part of this special team, she seemed very receptive. I was expecting a "Yes, you are on the team" response, but I knew it could not be that easy.

She mentioned that they get many requests from individuals wanting to be on the team, and if I was really interested, then I would have to contact a law firm in San Diego, California, who overlooked the selection process of the team. I would also have to write an essay as to why I wanted to be on the team. I was encouraged as I talked to this woman from Team Hoyt, because from my past experience, whenever I announced a dream to someone I was usually greeted by words of discouragement—but not this time. As I hung up the phone, a feeling of fear came over me. I have to write an essay? Essays are hard work. I always found that the hardest part in writing an essay was writing the first word. What would I say? How would I begin this ever-so-important task? I knew this essay would be crucial in the selection process, so I would have to choose my words carefully. It would have to be insightful and thought-provoking. The task seemed daunting as I sat at my computer. As I stared at my computer screen, I remembered the word that started my entire journey off for me just a few years before. *Can.* Then it happened. The words slowly started to take shape on the paper as I thought, *I can do this, and I can do it well.*

As I continued to write, I found myself having a severe case of diarrhea of the mouth. I couldn't stop. It was as if the words just appeared on the screen as I found myself editing my essay several times, until I thought it was ready to send off. As I clicked the *send* button on my email, I knew it was in God's hands.

I have been known to be an impatient person at times, and as I sat at the computer, staring at my email, I found myself, in union with each beat of my heart, clicking on the *receive mail* button, repetitively waiting in anticipation for a reply to come back. I knew it could take hours or even days, but I was not going to miss this email.

It would be only a matter of hours later when I would receive a response back from this law firm in California. I was pumped and energized to read that they had received my email and were going to review my essay. I was ready to run to California from Canada and wait in the waiting room to get their official response.

Then it happened. An email from Team Hoyt appeared in my inbox, stating that I had been selected to run with Team Hoyt in the Boston Marathon in April of 2012. Words would never be able to explain my excitement in that moment. It was as if I had won the lottery. Not only was I going to run the Boston Marathon as a qualified runner, I was going to run it with Team Hoyt. The email went on to explain that this was going to be a special year for Team Hoyt, as this would be Dick and Rick's 30th running of the Boston Marathon, and what a party it was going to be. I wanted to reach through the computer and give Kathy a hug for making my day, but I knew I would be able to do that in person one day soon.

A splash of cold water awakened me from my thoughts as I glanced down on my singlet to read those very words which were stitched into its fabric: "Team Hoyt." My fourth dream had been accomplished!

The heat was starting to get unbearable as I passed the 10-kilometer marker. It felt like the road underneath was starting to melt as I pushed into it. I now felt the painful effects of the heat, and I knew the journey had just begun. Another 32 kilometers lay in wait as the runners ahead of me slowed their pace with each passing mile.

As I looked up, I saw Dick and Rick Hoyt just yards ahead of me. Rick's face lit up the crowd as they made their way along the route. And there was Dick, faithfully staying true to the course. Here was a man who committed himself, never once wavering to his calling in life. This patient, loyal, and loving father was giving of himself as the two of them shared the journey together. The cheers from the crowd pushed us along as they shouted, "Yes, you can!" As my thoughts drowned out the voices around me, I found myself thinking about the moment when I first met Dick and Rick just a few days before. It was a moment that I would never forget.

We were just leaving our hotel room on Saturday morning, as the streets of Boston were calling us to explore a whole new world. As we gazed through the shop windows, my world was put on hold again as my phone rang, notifying me that Kathy, from Team Hoyt, was calling. To my surprise, she informed me that both Dick and Rick had arrived at the Boston Marathon Expo and would be signing autographs. Dick would like to meet me, if I could make it to the expo. I was ecstatic! As I hung up the phone, my wife looked at me, waiting for a response. I tried to say the words, but nothing seemed to come out. The moment between dreaming and reality was here. I would finally meet the people who awakened my destiny—my destiny to run.

We wasted no time venturing off to the Boston Marathon Expo. The expo was full of excited and passionate runners. The energy inside the building was electrifying. It took us a few moments to orient ourselves to where the Hoyts may be. We would, of course, have to stop at every booth in the massive building, but that would come later. We were on a mission, and there was no stopping us now.

It felt like we were in a time warp as we blazed past all the clothing, shoes, and the marathon paraphernalia that the expo had to offer. As we rounded a corner, we finally spotted the Hoyts. They were exactly like we had envisioned. Their warm smiles welcomed visitors from all over the world.

As I stood there watching the people interact with the Hoyts, I reflected on my journey over the past four years. The journey had been long and hard. It had its challenges, but it also had its rewards, and this moment would be the climax of all the hard work. From a couch potato to a marathon runner, the journey had brought me to this place, and here I stood, frozen in time. I knew it was worth it all when I saw the smiling faces of those who interacted with the Hoyts. This was the moment I had been waiting for.

As I walked up to Dick Hoyt, I firmly shook his hand, and with a big, broad smile, I said those very words that I had been rehearsing for years. "Thank you, Mr. Hoyt, for inspiring me. You changed my life by your example."

It was a moment I would cherish for a lifetime as Dick Hoyt thanked me for supporting the Hoyt Foundation and spreading the "Yes, You Can" message. As we gathered for a photo, Dick said to me those very words that I long for God Himself to say to me one day. "Well done!" Dick's words made the journey worthwhile.

Pulsating pains from my toe awaken my thoughts as I realized I had just lost my first toenail, which lodged in my shoe. Not wanting to lose any time in stopping, I pushed aside the newest of souvenirs I inherited from this run. One of the most hated enemies of long-distance runners is wet shoes. They can cause terrible problems for feet, including painful blisters, among other things. As I looked up, I realized I had finally reached the 16-kilometer marker, and I knew the other 26 kilometers would produce other keepsakes as I pushed on toward my next drop of water.

I could always tell where the next watering hole was by the amount of people gathering around it, for it looked more like the trading floor of the New York Stock Exchange, as patrons waved their arms grasping at every attempt to get the water they so desperately needed. Water had become a valuable commodity as runners pushed their way to the table to make their trade, their precious time for a drink of water.

As I took several cups of water to soothe my parched throat, I felt a hand come upon me from one of my Team Hoyt members. It was a touch of encouragement, and we both smiled and headed for the next water station a mile ahead. In that moment, I realized what true friends I had made in just a few short days, as over forty runners came together to form this amazing team called Team Hoyt.

It was just two days ago when I sauntered into the food court at a mall to meet the members of Team Hoyt. This was our first team meeting, and there was excitement in the air as I walked toward the crowd. There was something special about this team, I felt. Although strangers, there was a kindred spirit that drew us together. There was unity in the room as we introduced ourselves and shared our stories. These stories all had one common thread woven throughout it and that was the message of "Yes, You Can." I know that everyone has a story to tell, but in that room I sat spellbound as the tears, laughter, and hugs made this team a family. As I left the team meeting, I was energized, as we would journey together in uncharted waters, as a team, for the next forty-eight hours.

I couldn't help but wonder if that was what heaven would be like.

People laughing, sharing, hugging, and supporting each other. There were no words of negativity or criticisms, not even gossip or rumors would be heard as we shared our stories. It was a powerful moment that reminded me that, yes, anything is possible. We had come together for a common purpose, and that is what motivated us to do the impossible. Our common purpose is what lit our passion to strive to encourage each one, and it was that passion that would get us to the finishing line. I wondered if this is what Jesus meant with He came to give life and to give it abundantly. This was definitely the abundant life.

A distant thunder was heard, as I was a mile from the halfway point of the marathon. A smile came over my face as I looked at my teammate. As a rookie looking at his experienced partner, my Team Hoyt friend said, "Get ready. You will never forget this next mile coming up!" I was warned about this part in the race where every runner would hear their ears ring for miles afterward. We were approaching Wellesley College.

Wellesley College is a private women's liberal-arts college known for its strong academic standing, as well as for its world-famous support given to runners during the Boston Marathon. Thousands of girls would line up along the route in front of Wellesley College and do what they do best: cheer us on.

I am a father of four teenage daughters, and the decibel level in our home can get to an ear-piercing level at times. *Maybe that's why I run*, I thought. Like making your way to the stage in a rock concert, with each step we took, the distant thunder soon turned into an ear-deafening roar as we were about to enter what was once known as the "screaming tunnel," the screaming girls from Wellesley College.

Today, the college had a stronger-than-normal crowd showing their creative signs and offering plenty of positive energy, pushing the runners toward Boston. This was the shortest mile I had ever run along, and I floated along their cheers and high-fives, as this was a much-needed distraction as we prepared ourselves for yet another grueling 13.1 miles.

The time was now nearing high noon. With not one shade tree along the run, the sun had become our constant friend, or foe. The temperature now peaked in the high eighties, and there was no stopping it. My mind was starting to play tricks, as I saw puddles form on road ahead. Like in a desert walk, mirages of water started appearing on road ahead. The heat continued to rise from the roadway, causing many runners to become disoriented and slow down their pace considerably. These mirages brought me hope that water was just ahead as I pushed on toward each mirage.

A savage blast of hot air broke free as I ran past an alleyway between two buildings. Like a hair dryer on full blast, I found myself disoriented for a moment as I tried to regain my composure. As I zoned back in, I realized my journey was now half over.

"Go Team Hoyt!" was shouted by dozens of people as I rounded a corner. With their fists pumped in the air, I felt my pace quicken as they shouted, "Yes, you can!" Cheers erupted in the crowd as people pointed to my Team Hoyt singlet. As I ran by the crowd, I could hear a familiar voice in my mind; it was words of encouragement from our coach and friend Uta Pippig.

Uta was our team coach, and she would often call me up in the months leading up to the marathon, encouraging me in my training and offering tips to enhance my training. I truly felt humbled as I realized that Uta was more than a three-time Boston marathon winner, an Olympic runner for Germany, and a face for Nike commercials; she was an encourager and an inspiration to all of us. She made time for us all, and I felt privileged to talk with her for hours on the phone.

I had just met Uta in person two days earlier during our Team Hoyt reception dinner. She was the person whose voice I knew. but whose face I had never seen in person. As Uta walked into the room, that ever so famous smile was seen on her face: a smile that would light up the room and send rays of hope and excitement throughout the crowd. She had done something for each of us; she had made a difference in our lives. As I approached her, her arms went outstretched for the warm hug that once again said, well done!

As the dinner reception continued, I turned around, and to my amazement, the famous Bill Rodgers walked in. The legendary runner whom I read about and had seen on TV was now encouraging all of us to run for the prize. This icon, once the former marathon record-holder, winner of the Boston and New York Marathons and inductee into the U.S. Track and Field Hall of Fame, was now in the room. It was as if I was watching a movie, but this movie was reality, and I was blessed to experience all this.

I looked down at my watch as I neared the famous heartbreak hill. My pace was much slower than anticipated, and the thought of setting my personal best in this race was a distant memory. The officials were right when the warned that today's pace would be much slower than the years before.

As I stopped at the water table, my legs started to burn with pain. The constant pounding of my legs in the midday sun had taken its toll on me. I found that, with each new stop at the watering hole, a whole new talk was heard among the crowd. The talk at this table not only shocked me, but made me realize just how blessed I was to still keep running.

The rumor was true. Kenya's Geoffrey Mutai, the defending champion of last year's record-shattering win, dropped out of the race at this very mark: the 18-mile mark. Just the year before, Kenya's Geoffrey Mutai had set a record shattering run with a finishing time of 2:03:02. Geoffrey's first place finish that year would earn him a check for $225,000 for his valiant and speed-breaking run, but not this year! As I pushed off from the table, I knew I had to prepare myself for the biggest challenge of the race yet, Heartbreak Hill.

I could tell I was nearing it as I saw runners starting to slow to a walk. As a new runner to the Boston Marathon, I was excited to take on this famous hill. I had heard so much about it, watched it on TV as a child, and now the dream was here. I was soon to be on Heartbreak Hill! I was ready to take on Goliath! With each step closer to the hill, I could hear its challenge: walk, do not run!

I was determined more than ever not to yield to its threatening intimidation. Like a bully shouting in the school yard, I was ready to take it on. Heartbreak Hill is an ascent over .4 miles between the 20- and 21-mile mark. As I made my way over to meet the hill, I couldn't help but recall the time I collapsed in a 10-kilometer race two years earlier. Could it be that this hill would win, causing me to stumble, and not get back up? If I was going to collapse, I knew it would be around this point. For up at the top of the hill awaited the wall, the point where energy reserves were now depleted.

I laughed to myself as I started running up the hill, as I remembered that my doctor was running right behind me in this race. A wave of assurance came over me as I recalled my conversation with him just twenty-four hours earlier at the Boston Marathon expo.

As I took in all the sights around me at the expo, I had spotted a very familiar person in the sea of faces that walked by us. His name is Dr. Ken Walker. Ken lives just a few miles from me in Canada, and it was nice to see a familiar face from my home town. Ken was my doctor for many years and a good friend. Ken, an avid marathon runner, running over sixty marathons, had encouraged me during my past four years. I would often meet him on my long runs, and his smiles and words of wisdom would inspire me to run faster and push harder. As we talked about the heat, Ken, knowing that I had collapsed in a 10-kilometer race in my hometown, offered some hope to me when he said that, since I was a faster runner than he was, if I was to collapse on the run due to the extreme heat, as a doctor he would do something for me as he passed me, he would get down and stop my Garmin watch and then continue running on. Like a true runner, that's all I wanted to hear from him. Time stops when you collapse, and I appreciated Dr. Walker's concern for me and my well-being.

As we laughed about stopping time on my Garmin, Dr. Walker then offered an inspiring word to me that would change my outlook. "Instead of running for time," he offered, "run to beat your bib number." I paused and at that moment I realized he was right! I would set a new goal now, one based not on time, but to beat my bib number. Was that doable, to beat this number?

Boston bib numbers are among the most special of numbers. Bib numbers are assigned according to your qualification time. The lower the bib numbers the faster the runner you are. It is a ranking system that would see runners categorized by their speed. Since my bib number was 6287 that placed me in the top third of the race. I felt privileged to be up near the front of the race, but humbled to be blessed by God for allowing me to be here. Dr. Walker was right. The goal now was not to make my personal best time, but rather to beat my bib number! I believed it was quite doable, and I was determined to do it. That moment for me was a God moment. It changed my lookout and how I was going to run the race. The odds of meeting Ken at the precise moment were incredible, but I knew this was a word from God.

An audible laugh was heard from me as I looked up and realized I had already conquered the hill. With only 10 kilometers left, I was on my way home. I had done the impossible. I had conquered Goliath, and there was no stopping me. I could now see the glorious city of Boston, with its skyscrapers welcoming me into the city. It truly was a sight to behold. The race was soon coming to an end.

At that moment, I could hear my wife's voice in my mind telling me not to get too overconfident at this point in the race. Marathon runners know that the second half of the marathon usually begins at the 32-kilometer mark, making the last 10 kilometers seem unbearable and long. I still needed to run smart, and anything could happen still. Her soothing voice reminded me that she was right. She always is. I can be very stubborn at times, and this usually causes me problems that would eventually lead to the famous words, "I told you so." As I zoned in, a smile took shape on my face as I was reminded of an experience just days before as we entered the city of Boston.

In my excitement of the moment, as we drove closer to the city limits of Boston, we realized that our vehicle was moments away from being out of gas. With the streets clogged with cars, a Friday afternoon arrival time was not the best time to go on an excursion looking for gas stations. My wife had cautioned me to get gas outside the city, but in my infinite wisdom, I knew we could easily find a gas station in the city.

It would be a slow and laborious drive as we fought through the traffic to finally find a gas station, as our vehicle rolled to a stop, out of gas. We were relieved to find this place of refuge and solitude. Although this gas station resembled more like a used car lot rather than a gas station, in my desperation, I was willing to stop at any place that sold gasoline.

As I got out and looked across the road, there it was, Fenway Park, that beautiful historic park. The place where the legendary green monster lived in left field was right before my eyes. This place was mecca for thousands of loyal baseball fans, and here I was, standing right across from it. This landmark was calling my name as the aroma of the Fenway ballpark hotdogs permeated the air. *Now this is a city,* I thought. A city we would call home for the next few days.

With thousands of fans pouring out of Fenway Park, I turned to fill my vehicle up with gas only to be greeted with a sign that said "No gas." "No gas?" I said out loud to no one in particular. "A gas station in the middle of Boston, and no gas?" In my pursuit for an answer from the gas attendant, I was informed by a couple of motorcycle riders that gas stations do not sell gas during a game, but rather the gas stations near Fenway Park serve as parking lots for fans attending the game. Gas stations near Fenway Park make more money selling parking spots than they do selling gas, so they shut down their pumps while the game is being played.

I couldn't believe it. With places to go and things to do, would we have to wait until the game was over to get gas? My enthusiasm for the city soon dissipated into disappointment. As I stood in my confusion, my negative attitude was getting the best of me, and that needed to change. It would only be a matter of seconds when the gas attendant would tell me that I could start pumping gas.

My wife was right, as I heard someone shout from the crowd, "What are you laughing about?"

It must have been a strange sight for the crowd to see a runner laughing at this point in the race, considering that most runners were in pain and doing everything they could to push themselves to the finishing line.

"My wife is right!" I shouted. I couldn't believe I had said and even admitted to that. Several confused stares were shared with the crowd, and I observed one lady nodding her head to her husband. My wife was right, I needed to run smartly.

With each step, I could feel the vibrations of the crowd at the finishing line. I was now within striking distance of finishing the marathon. A feeling of indescribable excitement came over me as I prepared myself for one of my greatest moments in my life, crossing the finishing line at the Boston Marathon, my dream come true.

I could hear the crowd at the finish line as I rounded the corner to head for the home stretch, Boylston Street. I was looking for my family in the crowd. They were waiting there patiently for me and, like a hawk, I was scanning the crowds looking for them. I would recognize them by the Canadian flag being waved over their heads. And then I spotted it— my family with the biggest smiles and cheers handed me the Canadian flag as I turned for the finish line. With the flag in my hand, I ran toward the finish line with my head held high. The thunderous applause and screaming would awaken energy within me that I did not know I had. With all my effort, I ran towards the prize, the prize that awaited all of us who endured to the end, the precious Boston Marathon finishers' medal.

I had done it, with at time of 3:36:10 and placing 3,911th out of over 22,000 runners, I had beaten my bib number. With pain radiating from my entire body, there was no greater joy than stepping on the finish line. I was reminded of what Paul said in the New Testament, as the medal was placed around my neck that, "Do you not know that in a race all the runners run, but only one gets the prize? Run in such a way as to get the prize," (I Corinthians 9:24). That prize was now in my hand. Even though I did not achieve my personal best, I found myself saying that running, like life, is not all about time, but about our experiences along the way. I had incredible experiences during the past 26.2 miles and during the past four years.

This marathon would go down in the record books, as over 2,100 runners were treated for dehydration and exhaustion. Over 100 runners would be sent to the hospital for treatment, and over 1,000 runners would be treated at the finishing line.

As I made my way back to the hotel, hundreds of spectators would congratulate me on an incredible run. I thanked the Lord for allowing me to experience one of my greatest dreams, running the Boston Marathon. There was a magical sparkle in my eye as I strolled down the streets, a sparkle that said *life is a gift, make a difference.* Maybe it was my Canadian personality, but as each person passed by me on the streets of Boston, a smile was seen extending from my face: a smile that would, in turn, invoke a smile in return. I always knew that if you give a stranger a smile, it might be the only sunshine he sees all day, and today the sun was shining. As I pondered the last 26.2 miles, I was glad I had made that conscious decision just four years ago to change my life. God had done the impossible, for together we set out on the path called dreams, and together we showed the world that you are never too late to become what He wants you to become. I was glad that I had started running and I was glad that I didn't do it alone. I followed after my Father. I found myself stopping at a street corner to ponder those very words, *following after God.*

Following after God, like running, is real and relatively simple, but it is hard work, and it isn't easy. It takes commitment, determination, perseverance, and dedication. Running can be challenging at times, but it comes with many rewards and blessings. Running allows us to make choices, like whether or not we take shorts cuts, or put minimal efforts into our workouts. We can even stay in bed on those days when we don't feel like it. It is those choices that bring us no rewards, but rather breeds regrets. Committing yourself to running brings risks, like getting cold, wet, or even too hot. You can even get hurt by tripping, or injury, or even an over-zealous dog chasing after you every now and again. There are numerous parallels that can be drawn from following after God and running, but as every runner will tell you, there is no greater feeling as to when you cross the finish line and you hear those words, "Well done! The victory is yours!"

I said a prayer of thanksgiving I also found myself thinking that I am never too old to become what I might have been. With that thought in mind, I knew adventures happen within you, and I was not done dreaming yet.

So, God, I have another dream. I want to become an Ironman!

MILE 130

Ironman, Here We Come

"You're doing a what?" Sue exclaimed in disbelief.

"I am going to do an Ironman Triathlon next," I responded to her proudly as we drove home from Boston.

As I looked at her, shaking her head in disbelief, I went on to explain to my daughters that an Ironman Triathlon is an event that consists of a 2.4-mile (3.86km) swim, followed by a 112-mile (180.25km) bike ride, and then a 26.2-mile (42.2km) marathon that has to be completed in seventeen hours.

"You're crazy, Dad," my daughters shouted in unison from the back seat.

As news spread around the community that a forty-four-year-old former couch potato and non-runner had finished the Boston Marathon, whispers were once again heard in abundance, but these whispers would be words of approval and praise. The naysayers were silenced as they removed themselves from the forefront. I knew it was never too late to be what you might have been. There would be no more *what if I had done that, or tried that?* When setting out on this journey, I knew the only failure a person could experience was the failure of not trying, and this thought lead me to dream big some more. I wanted to do an Ironman Triathlon, and then after that, I wanted to run as an angel for my Team Triumph. The possibilities of where my dreams could take me were endless.

The months of training and preparing for this ultimate endurance race soon diminished into days, and those days were reduced to just hours. I felt ready and prepared for the 140.6-mile journey that awaited me in Lake Placid, New York. I had seventeen hours to prove that anything is possible.

As I stood in the registration line at the Lake Placid Ironman check in facility, I couldn't help but recall my family's initial reaction when I had told them I wanted to do this competition, and here I was. My family has since learned that when I set out to accomplish something, I become determined to see it though, and this was one more example of that as they stood patiently beside me. This was all new for us. True, I was a marathon runner, but the world of triathlons was a whole lot bigger.

As we walked into a large gymnasium of a local high school, our eyes were wide as saucers as we saw volunteers working diligently doing a myriad of jobs. The start of the race would be less than forty-eight hours away, and hundreds of participants looked well prepared for the 140.6 miles that awaited them in the Adirondack Mountains of New York. And then I saw it, once my foe for so many years, had now become my friend.

"You are going to get weighed in, Dad," noted my daughter, as she pointed to a line that had competitors getting weighed in before the big event.

I had stepped on the scale thousands of times during my couch potato years, and now I could hear it calling me. As I fixed my gaze upon this device, I recalled my days as a lazy, 220-pound, all-you-can-eat type of guy, and here I was, getting ready for the biggest event in my life: the Ironman Triathlon. I found myself being drawn back to the day when the only running I did was running from the couch to the refrigerator and back, before the end of a commercial break.

All eyes were on the digital readout of the scale as I stepped on. The once-lightning-speed needle was now moved with ease as it reached its destination: 157.2 pounds, a far cry from the person I was just four years ago. I was alive, and here I was, ready to conquer the highest of mountains that surround this beautiful town called Lake Placid.

I had prepared for months for this one event. Running the Boston Marathon just three months earlier taught me to be ready for anything. I knew that competing in an Ironman Triathlon was quite different from most other triathlons that are shorter in length. This race would not only challenge me physically, but also mentally, emotionally, and spiritually. I had accepted pain as my fate, as I scanned the horizon looking at the mountain peaks that were nestled behind the world famous Lake Placid. The incredible hours of training motivated me to admit aloud, "Yes, I can do this!"

The Ironman Triathlon offers no mercy for those who had treaded lightly the roads before. This event demanded my utmost respect, and to finish this distance on any given day is a significant accomplishment. The word of the day would be "endurance." A substantial amount of endurance would have to be called up from the depths of my inner being, especially when it seems that I am all alone with just me and my inner thoughts screaming at me to quit.

The hour had now come, and thousands of spectators made their way to Mirror Lake to watch the starting of the swim portion of the race. As I hugged my family, I made my way through the maze of bodies that dotted the shoreline. I heard my daughter say to me, "You can do it, Dad.

You are an Ironman!"

Those words would ring true in my ears for the next thirteen hours. Though swimming was my least favorite of the three events, I still made my way to the front of the pack. As I treaded water waiting for that cannon to fire, signaling the beginning of the journey, I found myself mesmerized by the finely-tuned bodies that surrounded me. Like sharks ready to begin the attack, I was ready to join in on the pursuit. With an enormous explosion from the mouth of the cannon, the sharks soon turned instantly into a thousand piranhas all around me. It was white water all around. In the seconds that followed the start, I felt my head pounding from a kick to my head. My goggles had fallen off, and I knew I was in trouble.

The biggest mistake I made was to pause for a brief moment in time to grab my goggles. In that blink of an eye, I had three bodies on top of me, scrambling to get over me, with hundreds more behind them ready to make me shark bait. It was everything I could do as I gasped for air. In that moment, I cried out to God not to take me this far, only to fail at the starting line.

I found my goggles and put them on the best I could, as I fought my way through the pack. I was mad now. Even though I have a little English background in me, my fighting Irish took over. This was going to be my day, and I was willing to fight to the death to get through this part of the race.

I knew I had a black eye as I swam around the first lap. Not only was it stinging, I sensed my eye was a little puffy. A war wound I would cherish for the next few days. I laughed, as I thought I had done everything to prepare for this moment. I didn't realize that swimming was such a contact sport. I love being aggressive in sports, but aggression takes energy, and I found myself becoming exhausted as I closed in on the finish line of the swim portion.

As I made a valiant effort toward the shoreline, I found my sense of renewal when I saw my family cheering me on. Their screaming had made it all worthwhile as they held up their Ironman signs and shouted, "Yes, you can!" My goal was to do the swim in an hour and a half, and my face lit with excitement as I noted on the clock that I had achieved my personal best time as it read 1:19:16.

As I ran toward the transition area, I could hear the mountains behind the Olympic stadium inviting us to a distant world. As I mounted my bike and prepared for the 112-mile bike ride, a smile formed over my face as I figured I had over six hours of sitting on my bike seat. As a former couch potato, I have had ample experience sitting for six hours with a remote control in my hand, but the only difference was this time, this wasn't a couch seat, and I didn't have the bag of Oreo cookies with me, either. Just water and a handful of gels. As the course took us out of the village to the countryside, I found myself admiring God's creation as I headed off into the beautiful mountains.

The breathtaking ride through the Adirondack Mountains was overwhelming. With the sun reflecting off the streams that ran through the mountains, I was refreshed in knowing that God was watching over me. The steep mountains called for every ounce of power my muscles could afford to give, and the descents begged me to hang on as I raced at speeds I had never before achieved.

I found solace as I rode up and down the mountains. It was a time for me to reflect on what God had done in my life, and at times, I saw the strange glances of other cyclists looking at me as I caught myself talking out loud. The journey was long and hard, and it brought moments of doubt, pain, excitement, and joy as I battled the challenging elevation swings, tackled the steep climbs, and dodged many other cyclists who had fallen victim to the mountains' call of victory.

As I rounded one last corner that brought me back to the Olympic Center, in Lake Placid, I prepared for the pain that would follow, after sitting on my bike for so long. I looked up at the clock just in time to see that I had completed the 112-mile journey in 6:30:06. I had now conquered two of the disciplines in a triathlon and only one awaited me—the marathon run of 26.2 miles.

"This really hurts," I lamented to a volunteer who grabbed my bike as I ran off to the transition area. "This really hurts." Every fiber and muscle of my body screamed out in agony as I took those first few steps. My feet burned, and with each step I took, it seemed like I was stepping on a bed of hot coals. As I looked toward the mountains, I could see the marathon route, hilly and challenging. Running a marathon on a good day is challenging enough, but running it after completing a 2.4-mile swim and 112-mile bike ride gave a whole new meaning to running a marathon.

"I am done," cried a cyclist who had arrived in at the same time as me. "There is no way I can run that marathon, now." As we both limped off to the transition area, I thought to myself, *A marathon is a long ways. Could I really do this now?*

As I wobbled into the transition tent to change for the next event, I noticed dozens of athletes calling it quits, and in a moment of self-inflicted panic, I questioned if it was really possible to run a marathon, or if my dreams were a little too ambitious.

My fate was now before me, and I had a choice. I could quit, or I could persevere. In that moment of solitude, I was reminded of the word *can*. The video of a father pushing his son in the Ironman World Championship in Kona, Hawaii, flashed before me. In that instant, I heard that small, still voice that said, "Remember. Remember that race we did together? We can do this race together as well."

I remembered that race well. It was one of my most memorable races ever. The "Around the Bay" race in Hamilton, Ontario. It was a 30-kilometer run, and its claim to fame is that it is the oldest race on the continent, which was first run in 1894, three years before the Boston Marathon. Rich in tradition, it has been won by the best runners in the world, including the Boston Marathon winners and Olympic gold medalists. The race is run at the end of March, and many runners use this race as a prelude to the Boston Marathon in April.

I had not qualified for Boston, yet, but that qualification would come four weeks later. This race taught me that nothing is impossible and to dream big. This race is unique in that awards are based on time. If a runner could complete the race in less than 2 hours, a gold medal is given. A silver medal is given to runners who can complete this race between 2 hours to 2:15, and a bronze medal is given to those who receive a time over 2:15. Out of the 10,000-plus runners participating, only about 100 runners would ever meet the time requirement for a gold medal. About 250 people would receive silver, and the rest would receive the bronze medal.

As a new runner to the marathon world, I wanted to go for the silver. Very few people would ever receive silver, and I knew that if I wanted to qualify for Boston, I would have to aim for the silver medal. I had only been running for two years, and I was determined to run the race of my life.

With a population of just over a half-million people, Hamilton is located at the west end of Lake Ontario. It is known for its steel industry, and being near the lake, the cold north winds blow continuously. The day of the race was no different.

With a temperature of -17 Celsius (1.4 Fahrenheit), the cold winds beckoned us to prepare for the worst. Hamilton is built on a mountain and known for its hilly terrain. Although only 30 kilometers in length, this race would definitely prepare runners for the great Boston Marathon.

I had never run a race with so many people in it, but I knew my destiny awaited me. The first 20 kilometers was an exciting, scenic, fast route, but the last 10 kilometers includes rolling hills to the dreaded Valley Inn Hill, known as the Achilles Hill, positioned at the 25-kilometer mark. By the time runners reach this hill, not only are their thighs burning, but every part of their body is crying out in torment. Although the climb on this hill starts gently, a vertical piece of pavement stretches to infinity. Even though the hill is only a half-kilometer in length, it is a muscle-shredding climb that saps all energy runners have left. With hearts rapidly beating, runners find themselves walking to the finish line from this point on.

By the time I finished 21 kilometers, I was on track to finish with a silver medal. The only problem was, there was still the dreaded Achilles Hill. I prepared myself for the climb as I approached and gave it all I had.

As I got to the top of the hill, I found my heart rate telling me to start walking. I looked at my watch and in a moment of horror, I realized I would have to run the race of my life for the next 4 kilometers to get the silver medal. With a look of defeat, I knew this would not be possible. All my energy was gone now, and with each step, my legs cried out in pain. It was now just me and my music. I reached down and turned up my MP3 player and settled in for a long slow walk home. And then I heard it.

I could hear the footsteps behind me. A runner was fast approaching from behind, and it sounded like he wanted to race me. I couldn't believe it! How could he be sprinting at this point in the race? Not wanting to be outdone by this runner behind me, I starting racing him. Being a competitive individual, I was determined that he was not going to pass me. As the 27-kilometer mark approached I could still hear him, this runner would not quit, so I pressed on. As I approached the 28-kilometer mark, the footsteps were still right beside me, but by now I could see Copps Coliseum, the finishing location of the race. With his footsteps gaining on me, I sprinted like never before. With just 4 kilometers left, I knew I could beat this runner.

At last, the entrance to the Coliseum was upon us, and as I entered the Coliseum, I turned to look at my competitor, and to my amazement, there was no one beside me. In my confusion, I looked up at the clock that stood just 100 meters from me, and it read 2:14:37. I had 23 seconds to run 100 meters to win the silver medal, and run I did. I finished that race in a time of 2:14:50. I had done it, I had won the silver medal, and I knew at that moment, nothing was impossible.

That race taught me never to give up. As I looked back through all the race photos taken from the 26-kilometer point and beyond I wanted to see the face of the competitor who so daringly challenged me to that foot race, and in my total amazement, there was no one there. "It can't be," I said to my wife. "I heard the footsteps beside me the whole time."

"It must have been the footsteps of God," she said. "You were running with God."

The photos spoke for themselves; I was sprinting all by myself. What a strange sight that would have been for runners I passed during that 4 kilometer stretch. Coincidence? Was I just hearing things? All I know is that I would have never been able to succeed in achieving the silver medal if it wasn't for God pushing me. I never wanted to doubt His power again. I had the privilege to run with God, and that was an amazing experience.

As I took my first few steps out of the transition tent, I heard His small, still voice telling me, "Remember, we can do this together." As I grabbed a cup of cold water, I said to the volunteer behind the table, "There is no way I am quitting now. It's only a marathon."

As I ran out of the Olympic village into the mountains of New York, I found myself enjoying every moment. It was time well spent with God, as we celebrated the last four years of my life. This was my victory lap with God, and with each passing step, I found myself getting closer to the great finish line that awaited me in the Olympic Center.

I heard the roar of the crowd as I entered the Olympic speed-skating oval. Just 200 meters separated me from my ultimate dream, an Ironman. I knew my family would be watching, waiting there patiently as always, with their cameras in hand. They were my inspiration, and as I placed my arms above my head and ran down the homestretch, I heard Mike Reilly's voice, the voice of Ironman, confirming it over the speaker system when he said, "You are an Ironman!" With a run time of 4:59:00, I had done the impossible. From a non-athletic, overweight, unmotivated couch potato to Ironman. I had completed the Lake Placid, Ironman Triathlon in a time of 13:14:42.

"You are an Ironman!" my daughters shouted as they ran toward me. It was a beautiful day, a day that I would never forget. With my family in my arms, I said, "Thank you, God! Thank you for showing me that nothing is impossible and that 'I can do all things through Christ who strengthens me,'" (Philippians 4:13).

As I look back on that day, that day changed me. That event taught me that, regardless of the valleys and mountains that come in our way, we can still overcome them. Throughout the journey, there will be many who offer advice and insights on how you should live your life, but when it comes down to it, you must do what is right for you. Don't let the voices and whispers of others tell you what you can't do, but instead, venture out and see what is waiting for you. Follow your heart, and most importantly, don't live your life full of regrets. You have one life to live, live it to its fullest, and who knows, you might just stumble onto something great!

"Okay, God," I exclaimed, "for my next dream, I want to qualify for the Ironman World Championship in Kona, Hawaii."

"Not yet, my son," said God's still voice. "I have something better for you. I want you to write a book!"

MILE 140.6

Anything Is Possible –
Make a Difference

///

"Commit your activities to the Lord and your plans will be achieved"

-Proverbs 16:3

"Life is a journey, not a destination."

As I stand gazing at my chair, I am reminded that dreams do come true, and my story as a couch potato is now in the past. The path ahead awaits me. Life is a journey that will take us on many different roads. As you travel down these roads, you may see many other travelers. Some are heading in the same direction as you, and others are heading in the opposite direction. These roads all lead to various places, and as each fork in the road comes, we have a choice to make. We cannot take both paths at once, so we must make a decision as to which way we go. Do we take the road that looks the easiest, the one that will bring us the least resistance? This is the road that most people travel on, because it is safe and secure. It offers no promises, but brings many regrets. Or, do we take the road that is least travelled, which very few people ever dare to venture on? It is the road that brings adventure and excitement, but could also be unpredictable and filled with uncertainty. This is the road that brings hope and a future.

We all make choices, and as I sat on my comfy couch at the age of forty, I came to that fork in the road. I had to make a decision. Did I want to continue sitting on that couch eating my Oreo cookies while watching TV for the next forty years, or did I want to take a new road, one that would promise adventure, but could potentially bring hardship and hard work? Was I content just to exist and waste my life away, not ever making a difference in my life, or anyone else's? Would I be happy to come to the end of the road, look back and say to myself, "I should have or could have?" That would be a life full of regrets and disappointments. I was forty years old, and I knew there was more to life than the path I was on.

As I looked at road signs that labeled the paths, one sign pointed down the path called "The Road of Dreams," the other "The Easy Road." The road of dreams intrigued me, as this road had been the least travelled, because it brought with it risk and uncertainty. It was the unconventional road. There were stones on this road, and branches had fallen on its wayside. For good reason, it was the road less travelled. There appeared to be mountains in the distant horizon, and like a river, the road turned and wound its way into an unknown land. You could see the sun peeking over the mountaintops, and you see its beauty as you gazed down this road. The view was indescribable; the awe and wonder the road had to offer stood before me, but it was the road less travelled.

The road less travelled was spoken of by many travelers, and you ponder your choice. You heard their whispers as you stood at the fork in the road: voices that told you, "You will never succeed if you go down that road," and "You can't do that. It's impossible to travel that road." They discouraged you by saying that there is no hope of navigating its dangerous curves, for at times the road can barely be seen. But deep down you hear those words, "*Yes, you can* do this." That small, still voice says, "Follow me, and I will make your paths straight." The journey will require a step of faith, but it will come with many blessings.

The hardest choice you will make is taking that first step. The choice you make will ultimately determine your destiny. The road you take will determine who you are in the days to come. Life is a journey, not a destination. You have one life to live and you want to make it count. I am truly amazed how God uses people to encourage you along the journey. I am grateful that God used Pastor Steve Jones in that Sunday morning service at church, as he showed the Hoyt video to his parishioners. His message influenced me to make a change in my life. The choice was mine to make as to whether or not I would change my life.

As I slipped on my sneakers that cold December night, I made a choice, a choice that would take me on an adventure of a lifetime. I went out into the unknown darkness not knowing where the road would take me. I just ran, navigating the snow and ice. It was dangerous out, a place that no traveler was on. As I came back that night after travelling 5 kilometers, I knew I had made the right choice. That choice has made me who I am today, and I have no regrets about making that choice. It has brought me indescribable experiences and rewards, and as I look back down the road, I shout these very words to the travelers who stand at the fork in the road, wondering which road to take: "Live the dream! Don't let the dream live you."

As I share my story with countless individuals, I share with them that we all make choices, for we are the author of our own destinations. We all choose the path that we want to go down. I encourage you not to fall victim to those who would want to deter you from achieving your ambitions. It's time to move past those individuals who pull you down and hinder your goals.

I am reminded of a story that relates to life. One day, a farmer's donkey fell down into a well. The animal cried piteously for hours as the farmer tried to figure out a way to get him out. Finally, he decided it was probably impossible, and the animal was old and the well was dry anyway, so it just wasn't worth it to try and retrieve the donkey. So the farmer asked his neighbors to come over and help him cover up the well. They all grabbed shovels and began to shovel dirt into the well.

At first, when the donkey realized what was happening he cried horribly. Then, to everyone's amazement, he quieted down and let out some happy brays. A few shovel loads later, the farmer looked down the well to see what was happening and was astonished at what he saw. With every shovel of dirt that hit his back, the donkey was shaking it off and taking a step up.

As the farmer's neighbors continued to shovel dirt on top of the animal, he continued to shake it off and take a step up. Pretty soon, to everyone's amazement, the donkey stepped up over the edge of the well and trotted off!

The moral of the story is that you are the donkey. Life is going to shovel dirt on you. The trick to getting out of the well is to shake it off, and take a step up. Every adversity can be turned into a stepping stone. The way to get out of the deepest well is by never giving up, but by shaking yourself off and taking a step up. What happens to you isn't nearly as important as how you react to it. By God's divine hand, you were created for a purpose. Life is about becoming what God created you to be.

As an educator, I tell my students that there are three things that I never want them to forget.

> 1. God loves you. You are special. You were made by God's hands and in His image. He has a special plan for your life. God says in Jeremiah 29:11, "For I know the plans I have for you, declares the Lord, plans to prosper you and not to harm you, plans to give you hope and a future," (NIV). Regardless of what age you are or what situation you may find yourself in, God wants us to dream big.

2. "Yes, you can!" *Yes, you can* do anything you want. There will be many obstacles that come in our path, but with His strength, you can conquer life's struggles and challenges. Paul says in Philippians 3:14, "I can do all things through Christ who strengthens me," (NKJV). I have learned many lessons by watching the Hoyts: sacrificial love, determination, perseverance, and dedication, but the greatest lesson I learned is that "Yes, You Can." *Yes, you can* overcome the obstacles that might come your way. I am always reminded that when we are surrounded by what appears to be many difficulties, we may in fact be surrounded by many opportunities, and the Hoyts are a great example of this. Regardless of the opposition and roadblocks in life, you can do it. Dare to dream, and watch the impossible happen.

3. Make a difference! Life is not about me, but about serving others. We are all unique and given special skills and abilities. With those abilities, we can choose to make extraordinary things happen around us. The choice is yours. Even the simple things we do in life, like listening, or giving an encouraging word, can inspire others to do great things. There are so many things we can do to help one another. Once we take ownership of this term, great things await us, and there is much joy in giving.

The question that runs throughout the book is, "Can you trust God?" It wasn't until the age of forty that I was able to answer this fully and experience all that God wanted me to experience in this lifetime. It is ironic that, in the Bible, the number forty is used by God to represent a period of testing or judgment. The forty days and nights of rain during the flood (Genesis 7:4), the forty days of prayer and fasting by Moses and Jesus (Exodus 24:18; Matthew 4:2), the forty years the Israelites spent wandering the desert (Numbers 14:33-34), the forty days Jesus spent on the earth after his resurrection (Acts 1:3), and many other examples all point to this one question: can we trust God and rely on Him for all our needs? It took me forty years of testing before I realized that I was *Destined to Run* with God. Without God, I found, life makes no sense. God is not just the starting point in my life, He is the source of that, and I realize more than ever that my heavenly Father wants a relationship with me as we share the journey together.

Can I trust God? I can truly say, like Joshua, "As for me and my household, we will serve the Lord," (Joshua 24:15). I have done more living in the past few years of my life than in my first forty years. I have been blessed beyond measure, and I know this is just the beginning for me. The answer for me is a resounding, "Yes!"

I am "destined to run" for God. I long to continue to make a difference wherever I go, including with my running. People have asked me how they can make a difference by running. I respond by telling them that there are several ways of doing this. By your example, you can encourage someone to make a healthier lifestyle, or maybe be a running partner for someone, or even that smile on the roadway as you pass someone can go a long way.

This past year, I was introduced to a great group of individuals call *myTEAM TRIUMPH. myTEAM TRIUMPH* is an athletic ride-along program created for children, teens, adults, and veterans with disabilities who would normally not be able to experience endurance events such as triathlons or road races. The participants with disabilities are known as captains, and the athletes who have the honor of pushing and pulling the captains on the course are called their angels.

I have also had the privilege to be a part of myTEAM TRIUMPH, West Michigan Chapter, to be an angel pushing a captain in a 10-mile race. I found that getting involved with others takes on a whole new outlook for running, because it becomes less about me and more about others. There is no greater joy than seeing a disable individual experience the thrill of a lifetime by participating in a race.

After Rick Hoyt's first race with his father, Rick said to his dad, "Dad, when I run, it feels like my disability disappears." God can use your arms and legs to encourage someone and make a difference in their life. Why not begin today, and see what great things can happen, for anything is possible! Make a difference!

I do have one wish for all who journey down the road of dreams: dream big!

Best End Times

Ironman Triathlon — 13:14:42, 44 years old

Marathon — 3:11:02, 43 years old

30K — 2:14:36, 43years old

Half Marathon — 1:24:29, 44 years old

10K — 38:26, 43 years old

5K — 17:39, 44 years old

A NOTE FROM THE CROWD:
FROM PASTOR DAVE LANE

THE CHOICE IS YOURS:
WHAT WILL YOU DO?

As you have read this book, you realize that Wes doesn't draw his strength from his own abilities, but from a source far greater than himself. Many people would say that religion is a crutch, but for Wes, it isn't about religion, but a relationship. It is a relationship with his Creator, which has and continues to anchor him in his life journey.

As human beings, we long to thrive in healthy relationships. Because of that fact, God chose to interact with us through a relationship. But there are parts of this relationship that we must understand.

First, God loves us. God created us so that He could interact with us in a very personal way. The Bible tells us that God would come and walk with the first humans in the cool of the day. He did this not out of obligation, but rather a love for His creation.

Second, sin separates us. In order for a relationship to exist, there must be a choice. So God gave us the choice of obedience or rebellion. The first humans chose rebellion, opening the door for sin to enter the picture. Sin is anything we do, say, or think, that doesn't please God. There are two aspects of sin that we must understand. We are all born with it, and it separates us eternally from God. But this is not the end of the story. . .

Third, Jesus died for us. Because of God's deep love for His Creation, He to longed to restore His relationship with us. But the sin of man carried the penalty of death. So God was willing to make the ultimate sacrifice by allowing His one and only Son to take the penalty of mankind's sin. Historians tell us that Jesus willingly was crucified on a cross, not because of anything He had done. And what held Jesus to the cross that day weren't the spikes driven into His hands and feet, but rather His love for mankind. Jesus died and was buried in a tomb. But this was not the end, because on the third day, Jesus rose from the dead and conquered death, restoring our relationship with God.

For Wes, his relationship with God began with a choice to admit he was a sinner and believe that Jesus had dealt with his sin. Many see God as a dictator who demands loyalty. Rather, God is our Father who longs for a personal relationship with us. This is not a decision that is forced, but a choice that is offered. The decision is yours.

What choice will you make?

www.destinedtorun.net

Author bios

Wes Harding is a 1990 graduate of McMaster University with a degree in Religious Studies and a 2011 graduate of Windsor University with a degree in Education. He works as an educator at Temple Christian Academy and has gone from an overweight couch potato to Ironman in less than four years. In his spare time, Wes is a motivational speaker, encouraging people to live out their dreams because "anything is possible." He can be reached through his website at www.destinedtorun.net.

Todd Civin is a 1983 graduate of the SI Newhouse School of Public Communications at Syracuse University, where he earned his degree in Advertising Copywriting. Todd was born and raised in Spencer, Massachusetts, and currently resides in the town of Winchendon, Massachusetts. He is married to his wife of six years, Katie, and loves his "pride and joys": Corey, Erika, Julia, Kate, and Dakota as well as his grandchildren, Addison and Lukas. He is owner of Civin Media Relations, which promotes athletes, writers, and public figures and their creative projects. He serves as Team Hoyt's Social Media Director. He can be reached through his website at www.civinmediarelations.com.